Sunday School Specials 4

by Lois Keffer

Group

Loveland, Colorado

Dedication

"Because you are my help, I sing in the shadow of your wings.
My soul clings to you; your right hand upholds me" (Psalm 63:7-8).
Onward, Christian soldier!

Sunday School Specials 4

Copyright © 1999 Lois Keffer

Credits

Book Acquisitions Editor: Jan Kershner
Senior Editor: Dave Thornton
Chief Creative Officer: Joani Schultz
Copy Editor: Bob Kretschman
Art Director: Kari K. Monson
Cover Art Director: Jeff A. Storm
Cover Designer/Illustrator: Elise Lansdon
Designers: Dori Walker and Kari K. Monson
Computer Graphic Artist: Joyce Douglas
Illustrators: Jeff Carnehl and Lois Keffer
Production Manager: Peggy Naylor

Library of Congress Cataloging-in-Publication Data

Keffer, Lois.
      Sunday school specials.
      1. Christian education—Textbooks for children.
2. Bible—Study and teaching. 3. Christian education of
children. I. Title.
BV15561.K38   1992   268'.432   91-36923
ISBN 1-55945-082-7 (v. 1)
ISBN 1-55945-177-7 (v. 2)
ISBN 1-55945-606-X (v. 3)
ISBN 0-7644-2050-X (v. 4)

10 9 8 7 6 5 4 3 2 1   09 08 07 06 05 04 03 02 01 99
Printed in the United States of America.

Contents

THE LESSONS

The Armor of God

The Fruit of the Spirit

Celebrating Special Times

3

Introduction

The armor of God—what spiritual teaching could be more critical for kids growing up in what sociologists have called the post-Christian age? As I plunge into writing a fourth volume of *Sunday School Specials,* I've begun to see this passage of Scripture in a whole new light— not from insights gleaned from commentaries, but from my son. (As teachers, have some of you also learned your greatest lessons from your students or your own kids?)

I remember standing outside the school building with him on the first day of second grade. After a period of denial, we'd all finally come to terms with the Attention Deficit Disorder diagnosis. Because he was bright and not hyperactive, his fledgling elementary school career had gone into a tailspin before anyone had even noticed a problem. As Josh stood slumped against the side of the building, it was plain to see that school had become an enemy. The bell rang. Other kids dashed in. Josh remained still. Then all at once he straightened up, faced the school entrance, squared his shoulders, took a deep breath, and marched inside. I marveled at his strength of character. Then it occurred to me—*he's just put on God's armor!* He'd learned about putting on the armor of God from a study at our church's midweek club. That seven-year-old had suited up right before my eyes, bless his brave little heart.

Fast forward eleven years. Two weeks after finishing high school, Josh was off to boot camp. Grandpa had given Josh a small New Testament he'd carried as a chaplain in World War II, the same one that my older brother had carried in Vietnam. An early letter from Josh told how a Christian buddy had pulled him aside for a quick Bible study and prayer on a particularly discouraging day, and that they'd kept at it even though they were twice interrupted by drill sergeants. In the next letter, he requested a study Bible. When he received it, he wrote, "We call the little New Testaments 'daggers,' and whole Bibles are 'swords.' When my buddy saw my new study Bible, he said, 'Man, that's a battle ax!' " The armor of God was intact and the fiery darts of drill sergeants could not dislodge it.

Before the first weekend leave, he wrote, "There's a strip of sleazy bars called 'Victory Row.' That's where most of the guys are going. But four of us are going to a hotel on the opposite side of town so we won't even be tempted." Let's hear it for the breastplate of righteousness! And in Airborne school, when he took his first step out of a C-130 and into the clear blue sky, he reported, "My heart wasn't even beating hard. We prayed together, and I knew I was stepping into the hands of God." A ride on the shield of faith!

I share all that to say this: Teaching kids is a wonderful, sacred privilege, but it's not easy. Kids can—and do—push us to the limit sometimes. We wonder if we're making a difference at all. And we may not be there to see whether they ever pick up the armor of God and put it on. We may never know if they take bold steps of faith or if they stand strong in the face of temptation and evil.

Bless your hearts, teachers—many of your students will do just that. When you teach God's Word, you're building a legacy of faith that will stand forever. I'm so happy to be your partner in that effort.

In this new book you'll find a whole quarter's worth of creative, combined-class Bible lessons. Each lesson contains an opening game or activity that grabs kids' attention and tunes them in to the theme; an interactive Bible story; a life-application activity and reproducible handout that help kids apply what the Bible says to their own lives; and a challenging, meaningful closing.

This book includes sections on the armor of God, the fruit of the Spirit, and celebrating special times. The hands-on, active-learning techniques make it easy for you to capture and keep kids' interest. And you can be sure that the Bible lessons they learn will stick with them for a long time.

The Time Stuffers show you how to keep kids productively occupied before and after class and during their free moments. And you'll find special tips for gearing each Bible lesson to meet the needs of your particular group.

I'll be praying for you and your kids, that they'll put on the armor of God and that their lives and yours will spill over with the fruit of the Spirit.

Lois Keffer

Active Learning in Combined Classes

Research shows that people remember most of what they do, but only a small percentage of what they hear…which means that kids don't do their best learning sitting around a table talking! They need to be involved in lively activities that help bring home the truth of the lesson.

Active learning involves teaching through experiences. Students do things that help them understand important principles, messages, and ideas. Active learning is a discovery process that helps students internalize the truth as it unfolds. Kids don't sit and listen as a teacher tells them what to think and believe—they find out for themselves.

Each active-learning experience is followed by questions that encourage kids to share their feelings about what just happened. Further discussion questions help kids interpret their feelings and decide how this truth affects their lives. The final part of each lesson challenges kids to decide what they'll do with what they've learned—how they'll apply it to their lives during the coming week.

How do kids feel about active learning? They love it! Sunday school becomes exciting, slightly unpredictable, and more relevant and life-changing than ever before. So put the table aside, gather your props, and prepare for some unique and memorable learning experiences!

Active learning works beautifully in combined classes. When the group is playing a game or acting out a Bible story, kids of all ages can participate on an equal level. You don't need to worry about reading levels and writing skills. Everyone gets a chance to make important contributions to class activities and discussions.

5

These simple classroom tips will help you get your combined class off to a smooth start:

● When kids form groups, aim for an equal balance of older and younger kids in each group. Encourage the older kids to act as coaches to help younger students get in the swing of each activity.

● In "pair-share," students work together with a partner. When it's time to report to the whole class, each person tells his or her partner's response. This simple technique teaches kids to listen and to cooperate with each other.

● If an activity calls for reading or writing, pair young nonreaders with older kids who can lend their skills. Older kids enjoy the esteem boost that comes with acting as a mentor, and younger kids appreciate getting special attention and broadening their skills.

● Don't worry about discussion going over the heads of younger students. They'll be stimulated by what they hear the older kids saying. You may be surprised to find some of the most insightful discussion coming literally "out of the mouths of babes"!

● Make it a point to give everyone a chance to shine—not just the academically and athletically gifted students. Affirm kids for their cooperative attitudes when you see them working well together and encouraging each other.

How to Get Started With *Sunday School Specials 4*

Lesson Choice

The lessons in *Sunday School Specials 4* are grouped in three units, but each lesson is designed to stand on its own. You're not locked into doing the lessons in any particular order. Choose the topics that best suit the needs of your class.

Several of the lessons contain suggestions for using an intergenerational approach—inviting parents and other adults in the congregation to join the class. You may want to schedule these lessons for special Sundays in your church calendar.

Teaching Staff

When you combine Sunday school classes, teachers get a break! Teachers who would normally be teaching in your four- to twelve-year-old age group may want to take turns. Or ask teachers to sign up for the Sundays they'll be available to teach.

Preparation

Each week you'll need to gather the easy-to-find props in the You'll Need section and photocopy one or more reproducible handouts. Add to that a careful read of the lesson and Scripture passages, and you're ready to go!

Time Stuffers

What do you do when kids arrive fifteen minutes early? when one group finishes before others do? when there's extra time after class is over? Get kids involved in a Time Stuffer!

Each Time Stuffer needs just one preparation—then it's ready to use any time. Choose the Time Stuffer that best appeals to the interests of your group, or set up all three!

Rubber Stamp Basket

Buy an inexpensive stamp set or two—it's a small investment that will last for years. Ask families and teachers in the church if they have stamps they can loan you. Be sure to include stamps that have "guy" appeal. Place the stamps in a large basket with stamp pads, colored pencils, and paper. (The church probably has plenty of paper used on one side that it would be glad to share with you.) Set out the stamp basket and voilà!—kids will be happily occupied for several minutes.

Paper Wonders

Kids love paper folding and sculpture! Set out leftover photocopied handouts from lessons you've already taught. Kids will enjoy making extra crafts to give away to friends and to wow their families. You may want to make extra copies of all the handouts just for this purpose.

Vacation Board

You'll need a cork board, picture postcards, pushpins, and palm trees cut from construction paper. Mount the cork board at a height that's easily accessible to your youngest class members. Decorate it with construction paper palm trees and a few scenic postcards. Encourage kids to bring to class postcards, brochures, or drawings of places they have visited. Kids will have fun sharing their experiences and discovering what their classmates have been doing.

1 The Helmet of Salvation

LESSON AIM

To help kids understand that ★ God offers us the free gift of salvation.

OBJECTIVES

Kids will
- play a game that involves unequal trades,
- hear what Jesus offered the dying thief,
- make paper "helmets of salvation," and
- have the opportunity to accept God's forgiveness and grace.

YOU'LL NEED

- ❑ small prizes
- ❑ small boxes or bags
- ❑ pennies
- ❑ miniature marshmallows
- ❑ round toothpicks
- ❑ a CD or tape player
- ❑ a CD or cassette of soft worship music
- ❑ photocopies of the "Helmet of Salvation" handout (p. 15)
- ❑ scissors

BIBLE BASIS

Ephesians 6:17

"That kid just doesn't have her head on straight." How often have you heard that expression? It usually indicates that the child in question is mentally or spiritually

8

confused, displays wrong attitudes, and is otherwise generally discombobulated. As we "dress" our kids in the armor of God, let's work from the top down. Let's begin with the helmet of salvation and teach kids how to get their heads on straight! They need to understand that accepting God's offer of salvation means that

● they're forgiven. Thanks to Christ's redemptive work on the cross, their sins are no more. They're new creatures.

● they choose to be on God's side and to give God their loyalty.

● they choose to follow Jesus and to live as he did—lives that exemplify love and grace.

● they become heirs to God's kingdom and a glorious future in heaven.

Use this lesson to teach kids that accepting God's free gift of salvation is the only qualification they need to receive all the other great benefits that go along with being God's children. It's their key to the locker where all the other pieces of armor are kept, their first step into life in the Spirit with all its wonderful fruit, and their ticket to eternity in heaven.

Each denomination has its own expectations about how the step of salvation should be taken. Take time during this lesson to explain your church's view of this all-important process.

Luke 23:26–24:7

No Scripture more graphically illustrates the "unfair" trade that God freely offers than this conversation between Jesus and the dying thief who believed in him. Could it be that God loves humankind so much that when a thief who lives a life of crime professes faith with his dying breath, God will receive him? God will cleanse his heart and give him eternity in heaven? Absolutely!

UNDERSTANDING YOUR KIDS

As you teach kids these basic tenets of the Christian faith, be prepared for all kinds of responses. Some kids may reflect spiritual understanding far beyond their years. Some may display a hunger for God and a strong realization of personal inadequacy. Others may just be taking their first steps down that path. It's not always the oldest and brightest who are the most spiritually mature. You're the guide, and you're assisted by none other than the Holy Spirit. Use this lesson to teach kids that to put on the helmet of salvation is to step into the light of God's grace.

The Lesson

ATTENTION GRABBER

The Price Is Wrong

Before class, set out various small prizes on a table and hide each prize under a small box or a bag turned upside down. The prizes might include quarters, fancy pencils, erasers, or treats. You'll need one prize for each child, plus a couple of extras in case you have visitors. As kids enter, whet their curiosity about what might be hidden under the boxes and bags, but warn them that peeking disqualifies them from the game that's about to begin.

Have kids line up according to birthdays, the youngest in front and the oldest in back. Say: **We're going to begin today with a game. I'll give each of you a penny; then you'll have to decide if you want to keep the penny or trade it for one of the prizes on the table. If you decide to trade, you may choose one box or bag. There might be a good prize in the box or bag you choose, or there might be nothing at all.**

Hand the first child in line a penny and ask:

● **Would you rather keep your penny or have one of the prizes that's hidden on the table?**

If the child wants a prize, take the penny, and allow him or her to reveal one of the prizes on the table. The child must reveal only one prize, then take it and sit down. If the child prefers to keep the penny, simply have him or her sit down.

Repeat this process with each child. It will soon become obvious that all the prizes are worth much more than a penny. When everyone has played, gather kids in a circle and ask:

● **What did you think about this game?** (It was weird because the prizes were all worth more than the pennies; it was set up so we'd all want to trade our pennies for the prizes.)

● **Why do you think I'd set up a game where you all get better prizes than the pennies I gave you in the first place?** (Because you like us; because you wanted to make it fun; because that's what the book said to do.)

Say: **This game is called "The Price Is Wrong" because you all had a chance to trade for something much better than your pennies. Today we're going to find out how God offers us a trade that's even better than the trades I offered you in our game. We're going to learn that God offers us the free gift of salvation.**

Have children eat their treats or set their prizes aside so they won't be a distraction during the rest of the class.

BIBLE STUDY

The Sweet Gospel Story (Luke 23:26–24:7)

Say: **To begin today's Bible story, everyone needs to make a marshmallow**

TEACHER TIP

If you use edible prizes, it's best to make all the prizes edible so that everyone has a treat to enjoy.

---

man. I'll pass around a box of toothpicks and a bag of miniature marshmallows. Everyone take three toothpicks and five marshmallows. You may eat one of the marshmallows. Pass around the toothpicks and marshmallows.

When everyone is ready, say: **OK, let's make our marshmallow men together.** Demonstrate as you give the following instructions. **First, push a toothpick into a marshmallow. The marshmallow is a foot; the toothpick is a leg. Now make a second foot and leg. Hold the tops of the legs together and slide on two marshmallows—one for the body and one for the head. Now break your last toothpick in half and push the halves into the body to form arms. Great! Now you each have a marshmallow man. Set it on the floor in front of you, and sit on your hands.** Ask:

● **How do you feel about your marshmallow man? Do you like it or care for it at all?** (Yes, it's cute; no, I think it's dumb.)

● **Suppose I got really mean and walked around the circle and stepped on each person's marshmallow man. How would that make you feel?** (Angry; sad; I wouldn't want it to get spoiled.)

● **Suppose your marshmallow man suddenly came to life, walked up your arm, and poked you in the eye? How would you feel about it then?** (I'd be mad; I'd laugh; I'd punch it.)

Say: **You see, in some ways we're like our marshmallow men. God made us and he loves us and cares about us a lot—much more than we care for our marshmallow men. But we have an enemy—Satan. Sometimes Satan does mean things to us—like if I went around the circle and stomped on your marshmallow men. Satan always tries to get us to mess up and do wrong things. Sometimes we do. We may lie or cheat or steal or be disrespectful to our parents or even to God. Some of you said you wouldn't like it if your marshmallow men poked you in the eye and hurt you. God doesn't like it when we do things that are hurtful to him.** Ask:

● **What are some of the things we do that are hurtful to God?** (Use his name to swear; be mean and selfish; disobey the Ten Commandments.)

Say: **Our God is holy and perfect. When we sin and do things that are wrong, it's as though we are turning our backs toward God. Our sin separates us from our holy God. To show that, let's put our marshmallow men behind our backs.** Put your marshmallow man behind your back.

But God loves us and misses us all the time we are separated. So, to fix our broken relationship, God decided to give us an incredible gift—a gift that is worth much more than anything we could ever trade. God gave us the gift of his Son, Jesus. Jesus was a human being like us. But Jesus was much more than we are. He was both God and man. So, just like God, Jesus was perfect. He was tempted by Satan, but he never did any of the mean or wrong things that we do. He lived on earth to show us how we should live. He taught that loving God and loving others are the most important things in life.

After Jesus had taught and preached and healed people for almost three years, he paid for our sins by giving his own life. Jesus loved us so much that he was willing to do anything to fix our relationship with God. He took the punishment that we earned.

Use extra toothpicks to make three crosses side by side on the floor in front of you to represent Jesus and the two men who were crucified with him.

Roman soldiers hung Jesus on a cross to die. Two other men were put on crosses beside Jesus. They were both criminals. One of the criminals taunted Jesus and made fun of him. "Aren't you the Christ?" he asked. "Save yourself and us!"

But the other thief couldn't believe his ears. He could see that Jesus was someone special. Listen to what he said. Read Luke 23:40-42 aloud. Say: **What a thing to ask! This man was a criminal under a death sentence. And now, just as he was dying, he wanted Jesus to forgive him.** Ask:

● **Wasn't that too much to ask? Explain.** (No, because Jesus loved him; yes, because he was a bad guy.)

● **What did Jesus do?** (Forgave him; listened to him.)

Say: **Jesus could tell that this thief had faith in him. So, even though this man had lived a life of sin, Jesus turned to him and said, "Today you will be with me in paradise." Whoa!** Ask:

● **Was that a fair trade? A life of sin, maybe one hour of being good, then he gets to go to heaven?** (No, but Jesus did it anyway; yes, because the man believed in Jesus.)

Say: **Do you know that God is willing to make that trade with each one of us? That's right—God offers us the free gift of salvation. When we say, "God, please forgive my sins and make me clean inside and let me become Jesus' follower and live in heaven someday," God answers, "Yes, I'll do that for you. My Son Jesus paid for your sins, so now you can be my child. I'll love you and watch over you and guide your life. And when you die, you'll come and live with me forever in heaven."** Ask:

● **What do you think about that trade—our sins for becoming God's child and living in heaven someday?**

● **How is that like The Price Is Wrong game that we played at the beginning of class?**

Say: **That trade—that gift God gives us—is called salvation. It's a gift that God hopes each of us will accept.**

Take time at this point to explain your church's teaching about receiving God's forgiveness and free gift of salvation.

LIFE APPLICATION

Marshmallow Meditation

Say: **Remember the marshmallow man and how he was set behind your back to remind you that sin is like turning our backs on God? Because Jesus died, we don't have to be separated from God. You can bring that marshmallow man back out and take a look at it. Because of Jesus' great gift, we can come face to face with God. We don't have to be separated from him. I'll play some soft music as you pray silently. You may want to thank Jesus for being willing to die for us, you may want to thank Jesus for taking the blame for your sins, or you may want to pray for forgiveness. Let's spend a few moments in silent prayer.**

Play soft worship music as kids pray silently. Then close by praying aloud: **Thank you, Lord, for taking our sins and offering us the free gift of salvation. In Jesus' name, amen.**

COMMITMENT

Salvation Helmets

Before class, make a sample "Helmet of Salvation" from the handout on page 15.

Say: **When we accept God's free gift of salvation, we literally put on a piece of the armor of God—the helmet of salvation.** Ask:

● **What does a helmet do?** (Protects someone's head; acts as a second skull.)

● **What do you think the helmet of salvation might protect you from?**

Say: **Listen to what the Bible says about the whole armor of God and why we need it. See if you can identify how many pieces of armor there are.** Read aloud Ephesians 6:10-18. Then ask:

● **How many pieces of armor did you count?** (Six, plus prayer.)

● **What did you learn about why we need armor?** (Because we're on God's side in a battle between good and evil; because the evil one tries to hurt us.)

● **Why do you think the helmet of salvation is particularly important?**

Say: **God's armor protects us from our spiritual enemies.** Ask:

● **Who might not want us to be successful in our spiritual lives?** (Satan; people who are not on God's side.)

● **What might our spiritual enemies try to get us to do?** (Sin; disobey God.)

Say: **We Christians need to put on the helmet of salvation to protect ourselves. In upcoming lessons, we'll learn more about the full armor of God.** Put on the helmet of salvation you made before class. **These paper helmets can remind us of the real protection God's armor gives us.**

Distribute scissors and photocopies of the "Helmet of Salvation" handout (p. 15). Explain that kids are to fold on the dotted lines and cut on the solid lines, then gently stretch the helmets over their heads.

When all the kids have put on their helmets, say: **These helmets identify us as people who are on God's side in all spiritual conflicts. Now repeat after me!** Lead this rhyme as if it were a marching cadence, with the kids repeating each line.

**I don't know, but I've been told
The armor of God makes me strong and *bold!***

**See the helmet of salvation on my head?
God took my sins and gave me heaven instead.**

Then ask:

● **Besides heaven, what are some other privileges we receive by accepting God's forgiveness?** (Talking to God face to face; protection from spiritual enemies.)

Continue the cadence as a prayer:

Thank you, God, for these good gifts!

Help me live as you want me to live.

CLOSING

Ask:

● **What does it mean to you to put on the helmet of salvation?** (That I've accepted God's gift of forgiveness; that I'll live in heaven someday; that I'm a follower of Jesus; that I have eternal life.)

Say: **Good answers! Wearing the helmet of salvation also means that you are identified as a follower of Jesus, that he is your Lord and leader. Besides the helmet of salvation, there are several other pieces of armor for God's people. You can read about them in the verses printed on your helmet.**

Have kids take off their helmets. Ask volunteers to read each "ring" of the helmet aloud.

Say: **During upcoming lessons, we'll learn more about the other pieces of armor and how to put them on. If you enjoy memorizing, these are great verses to learn by heart. They'll help you remember all the protection you have as a person on God's side.**

Now I have an assignment I hope you'll accept. Show your helmet of salvation to someone this week, and explain what it reminds you of— that God offers us the free gift of salvation.

Make sure kids take their marshmallow men and their helmets of salvation as they leave.

Helmet of Salvation

Cut out the circle, and fold it in half on one dotted line, then in half again on the other dotted line.
Cut on the solid lines; then open the helmet, and gently stretch it over your head.

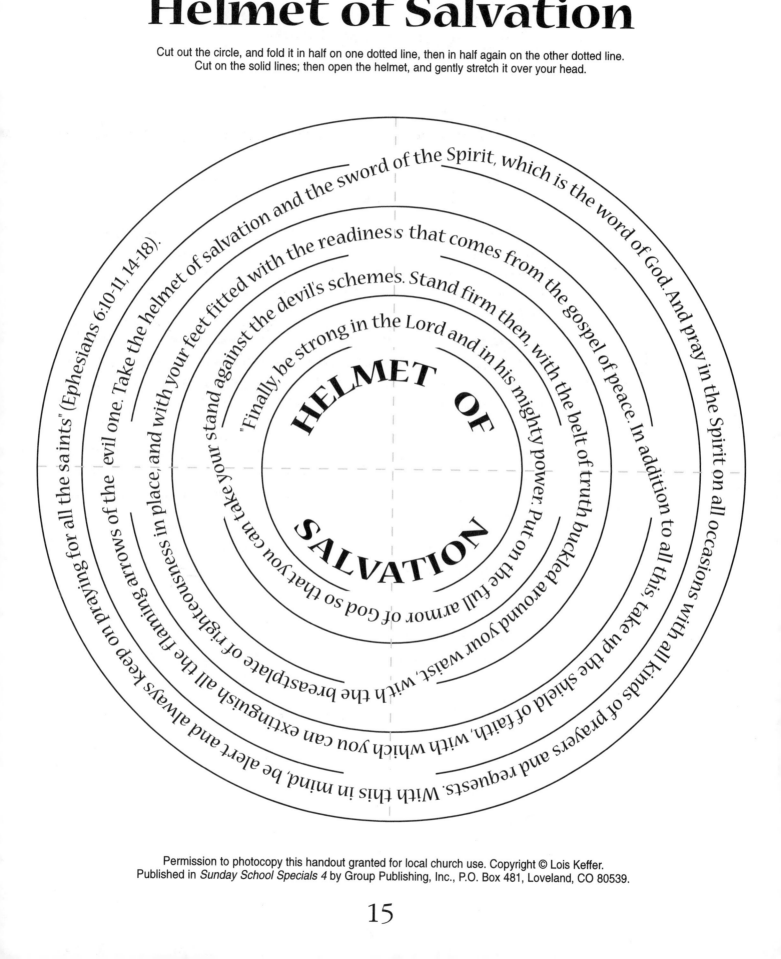

2 Breastplate, Belt, and Shield

LESSON AIM

To help kids understand that ★ God gives us his armor to protect us.

OBJECTIVES

Kids will
● play a game and try to knock each other off balance;
● learn how God protected Daniel;
● identify ways Satan might try to defeat them and how they can resist;
● make a commitment to wear God's armor by being truthful, doing what's right, and having faith in God.

YOU'LL NEED

❑ a photocopy of the "Quietest Lions Around" story (pp. 20-21)
❑ office paper used on one side
❑ photocopies on card stock of the "Breastplate, Belt, and Shield" handout (p. 25)
❑ disposable aluminum pie pans
❑ scissors
❑ masking tape

Daniel 6:1-28

Daniel distinguished himself among King Darius' advisers and thus became the target of his peers' jealousy. Consumed with the desire to bring Daniel down, the other rulers conspired against him. But Daniel was so pure in heart and actions that his detractors finally realized that they would never be able to discredit him unless they did it through cunning entrapment. So the snare was laid—they persuaded the king to sign into law a decree that for thirty days, no one should pray to anyone but the king. Violation of this decree would result in a one-way ticket to a den of hungry lions.

Now put yourself in Daniel's shoes. Would you have gone to a closet to pray, as Jesus suggested hundreds of years later? Would you have at least gone to an inner room of your house? Not Daniel. He knelt to pray in the window of an upstairs room where he could face Jerusalem. And the villains arrested him. But for reasons yet unknown to Darius, the lions lost their appetite at the sight of this godly man, regaining it when Daniel's detractors were lowered into the den. God's mighty power was at work!

Ephesians 6:14, 16

It sometimes seems that the world is a minefield for those who commit themselves to living godly lives. For God's people today, the best offense is still a good defense. The breastplate of righteousness prevented Daniel's enemies from finding any fault in his dealings. Because the belt of truth was around him, scrupulous honesty made him invulnerable to criticism. And when conspirators shot the fiery arrows of deception and malice, the shield of faith protected Daniel from all harm.

UNDERSTANDING YOUR KIDS

Kids from godly families often "stick out" as much as Daniel did. "No, I haven't seen that horror movie." "Yes, I believe God created the world." "No, you can't copy my homework." "Yes, I believe people should wait until they're married to have sex." "No, I won't lie to cover up what happened." "Hey—leave the new kid alone. He may be different from the rest of us, but that's no reason to make fun of him." Kids soon learn that the world doesn't always take kindly to people who live according to a higher standard. Use this lesson to teach kids that when they identify themselves as God's people, they'll probably meet with opposition but God will surround them with his care.

The Lesson

A Real Pushover

Say: **Let's begin today with a game. Find a partner who is about as tall as you are. Stand facing that person. Your feet must be together, no more than twelve inches from your partner's feet. Now hold up your hands and press them against your partner's hands.** Check to make sure all the pairs are in the correct position. **When I say "go," you may start pushing against your partner's hands so that your partner loses his or her balance. You don't want to knock your partner over—your goal is to cause your partner to get off-balance enough to have to move his or her feet. If you both end up moving your feet at the same time, start over. No hitting or bumping—you may only push your hands against your partner's hands. Has everybody got it? Go!**

After the first round, let kids find new partners and play again. Then say: **Go back to your original partners. We're going to play a little differently this time. Stand about two feet from your partner, and plant your feet wide apart. Press your hands together and try to push your partner off balance when I say "go." Ready? Go!**

Kids will discover that standing with their feet apart gives them much more control. They'll find it harder to push their partners off balance and easier to hold their own feet in place. If kids are enjoying the game, let them play it with two or three other partners. Then call time. Bring everyone together and ask:

● **Which way did you prefer to play the game—with your feet together or apart? Explain.** (I liked it with my feet together because it was easier to make my partner lose her balance; I liked it with feet apart because I could keep my balance better.)

TEACHER TIP

The second game is optional, but it's lots of fun and makes the point of the lesson beautifully. Play it only if you can take the kids to a carpeted or grassy area. And bear in mind these two simple precautions: (1) If you have a rough or hyperactive child, keep him or her next to you in line, and (2) arrange the line of children so you won't have any large children tipping in the direction of smaller children. I've used this game quite safely with large groups. If you choose not to use this game, simply jump ahead to the discussion questions after the optional section.

★ OPTIONAL GAME

Say: **We'll talk more about that game in just a minute. But right now, let's get ready for another game.** Lead kids to a carpeted or grassy area. Say: **Please line up shoulder to shoulder.** Place yourself at one end of the line. **I'll do a motion; then the person next to me will do it and pass it down the line. Then I'll do another motion and pass it down the line. Keep on copying my actions, and stay close to the people beside you.**

Lead the kids in these actions:
● kneel on your left knee;
● cross your right foot in front of your left knee;
● point far to the left with your right hand;

18

- point far to the right with your left hand;
- touch your nose to the inside of your arm.

At this point everyone will be twisted up and crouched close to the ground. Gently push the shoulder of the person next to you, and the whole line of kids will tip over like dominoes. It's a very silly feeling and a funny sight! Because kids are already so close to the ground, they just tip over gently rather than falling hard.

Let everyone enjoy a good laugh; then gather kids in a circle and ask:

- **What was it like to suddenly tip over?** (Really funny; a little weird; surprising.)
- **Why was it so easy for me to tip you over?** (Because we were all twisted up; because we weren't expecting it.) ★

Say: **Sometimes in life we get knocked off balance. Things creep up on us and surprise us, or we feel overwhelmed by things that are stronger than we are. Remember how much easier it was to keep your balance when I told you to plant your feet far apart? Well, God has ways of helping us stay on our feet when life tries to knock us down. God is stronger than anything we'll ever face. He gives us his armor to protect us. Let's see how the armor of God protected a famous Bible character.**

BIBLE STUDY

The Quietest Lions Around (Daniel 6:1-28)

Photocopy the "Quietest Lions Around" story (pp. 20-21). Before class, choose two students to be action leaders for the story. Let them read through the story and practice the actions given in italics.

Say: **Today we have two action leaders who are going to help with the story. As I read the story, I'd like you to *listen* to me, *watch* the action leaders, and *do* what they do. Got that? Let's go.**

If time allows, you may want to go through the story twice to make sure kids understand the plot. At the end of the story, have everyone give the action leaders a big round of applause.

Ask:

- **Why did Daniel have enemies who wanted to hurt him?** (Because he was their boss; because they were jealous; because the king liked Daniel best.)
- **Why did it take Daniel's enemies so long to bring him down?** (Because he was good and honest; because he never did anything wrong.)

Say: **Daniel had put on the armor of God (even though it wasn't written about until hundreds of years later). God gives us his armor to protect us. One piece of armor is called the belt of truth.**

go to Pg. 22

TEACHER TIP

A student who is physically active and enjoys lots of attention makes a good action leader. For the second action leader, choose a student who is outgoing and conscientious about staying on task.

19

The Quietest Lions Around

1. Darius was crowned king at age sixty-two.
    (Use hands to make a crown.)
    I think that's old for a king, how 'bout you?
    The king needed helpers to rule all the land,
    So he looked for some wise men to lend him a hand.
    (Strike a thoughtful pose.)

2. Darius chose helpers—a hundred and twenty.
    (Count on your fingers.)
    He thought a hundred and twenty was plenty!
    Then he chose three men who would help him the most.
    (Hold up three fingers.)
    Daniel was named to the number one post.
    (Hold up one finger.)

3. Daniel was glad to advise the new king.
    (Fold arms, smile, and nod.)
    With wisdom from God, he could solve anything!
    (Point up; then point to head.)
    So beside his window each morning and night,
    Daniel prayed and asked God to help him do right.
    (Fold hands and bow head.)

4. The king's other helpers were greedy, mean fellas.
    (Make a mean, snarly face.)
    Having Daniel in charge of things made them all jealous.
    They waited for Daniel to do something wrong;
    (Look at watch; then sigh and shake head.)
    Never has anyone waited so long!

5. They stormed, and they stewed, and they thought night and day.
    (Scowl and scratch head.)
    They'd get Daniel in trouble—there must be a way!
    They thought and they thought; then one said with a nod,
    "Let's get him in trouble for praying to God!"
    (Nod and shake finger.)

6. "We'll make a new law! Here's what it will say:
    (Pretend to unroll and read a scroll.)
    'People must pray to the king when they pray.'
    We'll get him to sign with the seal of his ring.
    (Point to ring finger.)
    Not a word can be changed. Not a bit! Not a thing!"

7. King Darius was flattered to hear this new deal.
    (Pat hair and smile.)
    He gladly approved it with his royal seal.
    (Press fist into opposite hand.)
    He was, after all, supreme ruler and king
    (Put hands on head like a crown.)
    And could tell all his subjects to do anything.

8. As soon as King Darius signed the new law,
    They went after Daniel, and here's what they saw:
    (March angrily; shield eyes and look up.)
    Daniel was in his house, down on his knees
    (Kneel and fold hands.)
    Praying to God, just as bold as you please!

Adapted from *Interactive Bible Stories for Children: Old Testament*, copyright © 1994 Group Publishing, Inc. Used by permission. Permission to photocopy this Bible story granted for local church use. Copyright © Lois Keffer. Published in *Sunday School Specials 4* by Group Publishing, Inc., P.O. Box 481, Loveland, CO 80539.

9 They dragged faithful Daniel off to the king
(Pretend to pull someone.)
And said, "He's been doing a terrible thing—
(Point and stomp foot.)
Praying to God! Now don't you forget—
The law says he must be thrown in the pit."
(Point dramatically.)

10 There was no way that Darius could save his adviser.
(Shake head sadly.)
He said sadly, "Daniel, I should have been wiser!
I shouldn't have listened to those evil men;
(Put hands over ears.)
May your God protect you in that lions' den!"
(Point upward; clasp hands together.)

11 The king woke the next morning and jumped out of bed,
(Open eyes wide.)
Threw his robe 'round his shoulders, his crown on his head.
(Pretend to put on robe and crown.)
He pushed open the doors and flew from his room.
(Run in place.)
He had to find out what had happened—and soon!

12 As fast as he could, the king ran to the den,
(Continue to run in place.)
Sure that the lions had eaten his friend.
He stopped, looked, and listened, but heard not a sound.
(Cup hand around ear; shake head.)
Those cats were the quietest lions around!

13 "Daniel!" he called, "did the God that you serve
(Cup hands around mouth.)
Keep you from being the lions' hors d'oeuvre?"

"Yes," Daniel answered. "I prayed through the night,
(Nod head and fold hands.)
And an angel shut all of the lions' mouths tight!"
(Put hands over mouth.)

14 "The great God I worship would never desert me;
(Raise hands and look up.)
Not once did those big, hungry cats try to hurt me.
(Cross arms and shake head.)
Not a growl did I hear, not a purr, not a roar,
(Cup hand around ear.)
Not a peep, not a sneeze, not a sniff, not a snore."

15 The king was delighted, and he gave a great shout,
(Raise fists in victory.)
"Come here, all you servants, and pull Daniel out!"
(Beckon; pretend to pull up on a rope.)
To all of the bad guys he said, "This is it.
Now it's your turn to go down into the pit!"
(Point forward; point down.)

16 Darius made up a new law right away;
(Pretend to read from a scroll.)
"Respect Daniel's God—he saved Daniel today!"
Then to the whole kingdom, they told Daniel's story,
(Spread arms wide.)
Worshipped the true God, and gave him great glory!
(Raise arms and look up.)

Adapted from *Interactive Bible Stories for Children: Old Testament*, copyright © 1994 Group Publishing, Inc. Used by permission. Permission to photocopy this Bible story granted for local church use. Copyright © Lois Keffer. Published in *Sunday School Specials 4* by Group Publishing, Inc., P.O. Box 481, Loveland, CO 80539.

Ask:

● **What evidence do you see that Daniel was wearing the belt of truth?** (He didn't lie to get out of trouble; he didn't hide his praying.)

Say: **Another piece of God's armor is called the breastplate of right-eousness. A breastplate is one of the largest and most important pieces of armor. It covered a soldier from his neck to his waist. Righteousness is living a life that is pleasing to God.** Ask:

● **What evidence do you see that Daniel was wearing the breastplate of righteousness?** (He followed God; no one would believe anything bad about him; everyone knew he always did the right thing.)

Say: **Daniel was good, honest, and godly, so his enemies couldn't find anything wrong with him. The only way they could hurt him was to make up a bad law.** Ask:

● **How did the bad law get Daniel in trouble?** (He prayed to God even when the law said he had to pray to the king.)

Say: **Even though the bad guys managed to pass a bad law, the shield of faith protected Daniel.** Ask:

● **What evidence do you see that Daniel was holding the shield of faith?** (He asked God for help; he prayed even though he knew he could be punished.)

Say: **Did you ever hear of hungry lions suddenly deciding that they're not so hungry after all? Daniel had faith in God, and God protected him so that everyone would know how mighty he is! The good news is that God still gives us his armor to protect us. Let's find out how.**

LIFE APPLICATION

Shields Up!

Have each child take scissors, a pie pan, and a photocopy of the "Breastplate, Belt, and Shield" handout (p. 25). As kids cut around the shield on the handout, distribute three two-inch strips of masking tape to each child. Let kids fold the tape into rolls and use it to attach their shields to the bottoms of their pie pans. Explain that kids can hold their shields by the edges.

Then say: **I wonder if you know how to put on these pieces of armor.** Ask:

● **How would you put on the belt of truth?** (By asking God to help you be honest; by always telling the truth.)

● **How would you put on the breastplate of righteousness?** (By asking God to help you do what's right; by asking God to forgive your sins; by trying to do what's right.)

● **How would you put on the shield of faith?** (By trusting God; by praying for God's help; by remembering that God is stronger than anyone or anything.)

Have kids form two groups. Give each group a stack of office paper that's been used on one side. Say: **Let's see how the armor of God protects us. The Bible tells us that the shield of faith can protect us from the flaming arrows of the evil one. In your groups, brainstorm how these pieces of armor might protect you from a particular temptation. For example,**

Jesus is truth

Jesus is our righteousness

Trusting that Jesus paid for our sins and is with us.

Jesus

you might be tempted to lie about finishing your homework—someone wearing the belt of truth would risk taking a zero rather than lie. Each time your group names a temptation, crumple a sheet of paper into a wad. I'll give you two minutes to brainstorm and make paper wads.

Visit both groups as they brainstorm, providing encouragement and ideas. Call time after two minutes. Lay a masking tape line down the middle of the room, and assign each group to one side of the line.

Say: **Let's see how your armor works. These paper wads represent flaming arrows of temptation. Group 1, you'll throw your paper wads at Group 2, and Group 2 will use its shields to block them. Is everybody ready? Go!**

After kids in Group 1 have thrown all their paper wads, have the groups switch roles so Group 2 throws and Group 1 blocks with its shields. When all the paper wads have been thrown, give half the paper wads back to Group 1.

Say: **Now you can throw and block at the same time. Throw any paper wad that's near you as you use your shields to block paper wads that come your way. When I clap three times, that's your signal to stop.**

Let kids play for a minute or two; then call time by clapping your hands. Have kids pile the paper wads in one corner of the room, then sit in a circle.

Ask:

● **How well did you protect yourself?** (Pretty well; OK.)

● **How does God's armor compare to the little shield you used to defend yourself?** (It's stronger because God is stronger than anyone; God's armor works better.)

COMMITMENT

Armor Rap

● **How can you put on God's armor each day?** (I can pray; I can ask God to be with me.)

Say: **It's important to remember that God gives us his armor to protect us. Let's learn three more verses of the "Armor of God Rap" that we started to learn last week.** Review the verses that kids learned last week by having them repeat after you in a marching cadence rhythm. Then add the three new verses.

I don't know, but I've been told
The armor of God makes me strong and *bold!*

See the helmet of salvation on my head?
God took my sins and gave me heaven instead.

Is the breastplate of righteousness on my chest?
Uh-huh! You can see that I'm wearin' God's best.

Is the belt of truth tied around my waist?
Uh-huh! I'm wrapped up in God's grace.

23

Is the shield of faith strapped on my arm?
Uh-huh! Satan's arrows will do me no harm.

Thank you, God, for these good gifts!
Help me live as you want me to live.

CLOSING

Armored Prayer

Say: Good job! You'll find the new verses to the rap on your shield. See if you can learn them this week. Now form a tight circle around me. Face outward, and hold out your shield as I pray for all of us.

Pray: Dear Lord, thank you for giving us your armor to protect us and help us stand strong. Help us to be truthful, to do what's right, and to have faith in you. Please protect each person here from all of Satan's attacks, and help us grow in our faith. In Jesus' name, amen.

Be sure kids take their shields as they leave.

Breastplate, Belt, and Shield

Belt of Truth

Is the belt of truth tied around my waist? Uh-huh! I'm wrapped up in God's grace.

Breastplate of Righteousness

Is the breastplate of righteousness on my chest? Uh-huh! You can see that I'm wearin' God's best.

Shield of Faith

Is the shield of faith strapped on my arm? Uh-huh! Satan's arrows will do me no harm.

Prayer of Thanks

Thank you, God, for these good gifts! Help me live as you want me to live.

3 Good News Shoes

LESSON AIM

To help kids understand that ★ God wants us to spread the good news.

OBJECTIVES

Kids will
- find hidden objects that tell about the life of Jesus,
- hear how Philip shared the good news,
- make Good News Shoes that tell the story of Jesus, and
- ask God to help them share the good news.

YOU'LL NEED

- ❑ straw or dried grass
- ❑ a small scrap of wood
- ❑ a sheep shape cut from white fleece or felt
- ❑ a Band-Aid
- ❑ a jewelry or paper heart
- ❑ a nail
- ❑ a small, round stone
- ❑ a small crown cut from foil

Note: If you'd prefer not to gather the above items, you may use the pictures from the "Good News Scrolls" handout (p. 34) instead.

- ❑ eight envelopes
- ❑ a photocopy of the "Philip's Visit" script (p. 30)
- ❑ a costume for Philip—robe, sandals, fake beard, and mustache
- ❑ scissors
- ❑ photocopies of the "Good News Shoes" handout (p. 33)
- ❑ photocopies of the "Good News Scrolls" handout (p. 34)

Acts 8:26-40

Many people confuse the Philip of Acts 8 with Philip the apostle. Philip the apostle was a resident of Bethsaida; the Philip of Acts 8, also known as Philip the Evangelist (Acts 21:8), lived in Caesarea. He is first introduced in Acts 6:5 when he was chosen as one of the seven who were to oversee the daily distribution of food. Because of intense persecution in Jerusalem, Philip and many other Christians were forced to flee. Acts 8:4 tells us that "those who had been scattered preached the word wherever they went." Philip went into a town in Samaria where he healed many people and drove out demons so that "there was great joy in that city" (verses 6-8).

The story of Philip and the Ethiopian eunuch certainly explains how Philip came to be know as "the Evangelist." An angel delivered Philip's marching orders to travel the road from Jerusalem to Gaza. On the road, Philip encountered an important Ethiopian official who just happened to be reading the book of Isaiah. When Philip ran alongside the chariot, the Ethiopian invited him to come up and explain the Scriptures. Before many miles had passed, the eunuch stopped the chariot so he could be baptized in acknowledgment of his newfound faith in Christ.

Even though we don't face the great perils that first century Christians encountered, somehow telling the good news has gotten to be bad news for too many Christians today. Why has sharing the gospel become a dreaded, onerous task? To put it simply, it is because we have an enemy whose flaming arrows fill us with doubt and cause us to shrink and hide. Will the person we're sharing with think we're weird? Will our little forays into really important issues earn us rejection or ridicule? Oh, if we could only step into Philip's shoes. What a runner he was—eager to speak of the wealth of God's love and the riches of becoming a child of God.

Ephesians 6:15

"You got shoes, I got shoes, all God's children got shoes..." Well, hallelujah! God wants us all to have shoes. Walkin', talkin' shoes. Shoes that carry us as we carry the good news of the gospel of peace. And it is *good news*. Through Christ, God offers to take our chaos, sin, and pain and give us peace in return. What a deal!

UNDERSTANDING YOUR KIDS

Nike. Reebok. Asics. Converse. Adidas. All God's children need shoes—and, boy, do they want brand names! If you've ever tried to get an elementary school child to settle for anything less, you're doubtless aware that such children invariably see your efforts to economize as the worst possible form of child abuse. Today, however, you can introduce your kids to a whole new category of elite shoes—shoes that transform the wearers into messengers for the King of heaven. Use this lesson to teach kids that, as exciting as it is to tie on those new Nike Airs, putting on the shoes that come with the armor of God is a much greater privilege—one that carries eternal significance.

The Lesson ATTENTION GRABBER

A Mystery Challenge

Before class, place the following items that relate to Jesus' life in separate envelopes: straw or dried grass (Jesus was born in a stable); a small scrap of wood (Jesus was a carpenter); a sheep shape cut from white fleece or felt using the pattern on page 34 (Jesus called himself the good shepherd); a Band-Aid (Jesus healed people); a jewelry or paper heart (Jesus taught us to love God and love others); a nail (Jesus took the punishment for our sins); a small, round stone (the stone was rolled away from Jesus' empty tomb); a shiny foil crown made from the pattern on page 34 (Jesus reigns in heaven). Seal the envelopes, and hide them around the room.

When kids arrive, say: **The first thing you'll need to do today is solve a mystery. I'm not even going to tell you what the mystery is about. But I will tell you this: I've hidden several clues around the room. The clues are inside eight sealed envelopes. When I say "go," you may begin searching for the envelopes. Each person may find only one envelope. If you find one, don't open it. Just come back to our circle, and we'll open them together after they've all been found. Ready? Go!**

When kids have found all the envelopes, gather everyone in a circle. Call on kids who are holding the envelopes to open them one by one. Each time a child opens an envelope and reveals what's inside, ask:

● **What could this clue be about?**

Accept all suggestions, and don't give any particular direction to the discussion until all eight clues have been revealed. Then, if kids haven't already guessed, ask:

● **How do all eight of these clues tie together? What could they be about?**

● **Could all of these items relate to a single thing or person? How?**

Continue asking questions and dropping hints until kids discover that all the clues relate to the life of Jesus. Then say: **Good work! You guys are super detectives. Today we're going to talk about telling others about Jesus because God wants us to spread the good news. Did you know that there's one piece of God's armor that's specifically meant to help us share the good news about Jesus? It's true. Let's meet a Bible character who wore that piece of armor and see how it helped him. On the count of three, let's call out, "Philip, Philip, come on down!"**

Count to three, and lead kids in calling out to Philip.

TEACHER TIP

If you're in a hurry to prepare the lesson, cut apart the pictures from the "Good News Scrolls" handout (p. 34), and place the pictures in envelopes in place of the actual items. To make the search more fun, use brightly colored envelopes.

BIBLE STUDY

The Gospel in Shoes (Acts 8:26-40)

Before class, arrange for a man to play the role of Philip and visit your class.

28

Give him a photocopy of the script, "Philip's Visit" (p. 30). Have him wait outside your classroom until the kids call out, "Philip, Philip, come on down!" Or play Philip yourself. Quickly don a robe and sandals. If you're a woman, stick on a fake beard and mustache—the kids will love it.

Say: **Philip seemed really excited about telling people about Jesus.** Ask:
- **Why do you think he was he so excited?** (Because he helped a man become a Christian.)
- **Have you ever had a chance to tell someone about Jesus? What was that like?** (I told my friend that Jesus would take care of him when his dad got sick; I invited my neighbor to vacation Bible school to hear about Jesus.)
- **Do you think telling people about Jesus is easy or hard? Explain.** (Hard, because people think you're weird; easy, because it's good news.)

Say: **The Bible tells us that it's important to tell people about Jesus whenever we can. Today we're going to learn how to do that. But we'll have to make sure that everyone has the right shoes on. Let me see your feet!** Inspect everyone's feet. **Nope—no one has the right shoes on. But never mind—I have shoes for you!**

TEACHER TIP

It's simple to make a beard and mustache from brown construction paper. Cut two pieces—one the width of your upper lip and two inches long, and another the width of your chin and three inches long. Cut narrow slits in both pieces to within one inch of the top. Curl the slit pieces tightly around a pencil. Apply the beard and mustache with tape that's sticky on both sides.

LIFE APPLICATION

Good News Shoes

Distribute photocopies of the "Good News Shoes" handout (p. 33). Say: **Believe it or not, these are shoes! They're Good News Shoes. They're part of the armor of God because God wants us to spread the good news. Listen.** Read Ephesians 6:14-15 aloud. Ask:
- **What do you think the Bible means by "the readiness that comes from the gospel of peace"?** (That we're ready to tell people about Jesus; that we want to share our faith.)

Say: **"Readiness" is an important word here. It means that whenever we're talking with people who need to hear about Jesus, we can jump right in and tell them.** Ask:
- **How do we know if people need to hear about Jesus?** (If they're sad or in trouble; if they've never heard about him.)
- **How did Philip find the Ethiopian man?** (An angel told him to go to that road; he heard the man reading from Isaiah.)

Say: **An angel of God told Philip to walk down that road, and Philip was on the lookout for someone he might help. We can be on the lookout too. Every day we can pray, "Lord, if there's someone who needs to hear about you, please help me find that person today, and help me tell the good news." It's really that simple! And these Good News Shoes will help you know what to say and how to say it.**

Before class, use an X-Acto knife to open the three slits in the shoe patterns. Have kids cut out the shoes and fold up (valley folds) on all the dotted lines. Show them how to slip the tabs on the "tongue" of the shoe into the slits on the top and how to slip the tab at the back of the shoe into the slit at the back.

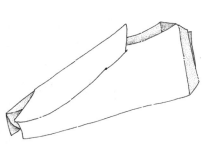

Philip's Visit

(based on Acts 6:1-6; 8:26-40)

When you hear the kids call, "Philip, Philip, come on down," rush breathlessly into the room.

Hi! Did you guys call me? I thought so. Well, it's nice to meet you. I'm Philip.

Shake hands with a few of the kids, and ask their names.

I guess you can see that I'm kind of out of breath. You wouldn't believe what just happened. Well, maybe you would believe it. After all, you're here in church, so you must know about the amazing things that God can do.

I've been working with Jesus' disciples for quite a while now. Not too long ago, the disciples chose seven men to help take care of church business in Jerusalem. They were so busy preaching and teaching that they needed other people to take care of poor people and do the everyday business of the church. I was one of seven who were chosen. Things got pretty hard in Jerusalem. We all shared our money and belongings, and that's how we took care of poor people. Then the Jewish leaders started making things hard for Christians in Jerusalem. Lots of our people were arrested and beaten—some were even put to death. So we had to scatter in all directions. But we pledged to preach the good news wherever we went.

Can any of you tell me what the good news about Jesus is?

Let kids share their knowledge of the gospel.

Hey, that's right! You guys are really on the ball. Good for you!

You know, people are really happy to hear about Jesus. Who wouldn't want to know that their sins can be forgiven and that they can become children of God and live in heaven someday? Talk about good news!

Well, back to my adventure. I was traveling through Samaria when suddenly an angel told me to walk down the road that goes to Gaza. So I did. And I saw a man who was an important government official in Ethiopia. He took care of the queen's money. Anyway, as he was riding along, he was reading the book of Isaiah. I started running alongside his chariot. "Do you understand what you're reading?" I asked him.

"How can I understand unless someone explains it to me?" he replied. Then he invited me to climb in and sit beside him. Whew—I was glad to accept. It's a little difficult to carry on a conversation when you're running!

Anyway, we talked, and I explained that Jesus died to take away the sins of the whole world and all we have to do is ask and Jesus will forgive our sins—then we can be children of God. This man was so happy to hear all this good news that he stopped his chariot by a stream and I baptized him right there. It was so exciting to see how much he loved God and how glad he was to have his sins forgiven!

Let me tell you, there's just nothing greater in this world than telling people about Jesus. And God wants us to spread the good news. I hope you'll share the good news every time you get the chance.

Well—I've got to run. There are lots more people like my Ethiopian friend who need to hear about Jesus. Thanks for inviting me to visit—I've had a great time. See ya!

As you run from the room, turn and wave at the kids.

Then say: **Now you need something to put in your shoes.** Distribute the "Good News Scrolls" handout (p. 34). Point out that the objects on the scrolls are similar to the objects kids found at the beginning of class. Let kids take turns reading aloud the verses written beneath each object. After each verse is read, ask:

● **Using this picture and verse, what could you tell someone about Jesus?**

Here are suggested comments for each picture and verse.

1. Straw in a manger—God sent Jesus into the world as a tiny baby.
2. Wood—Jesus lived with his family and worked as a carpenter until he was about thirty years old.
3. Band-Aid—Then Jesus began traveling around, preaching, teaching, and healing people. Many people believed that he was the Messiah promised long ago.
4. Sheep—Jesus said that he was the good shepherd who loved his sheep and that he would lay down his life for his sheep.
5. Heart—Jesus taught that the most important thing is to love God and to love others. He taught that those who love him will show their love by obeying him.
6. Nail and cross—Jesus taught that everyone has sinned and needs to be forgiven. He died on the cross to take the punishment for the sins of the whole world.
7. Tomb with the stone rolled away—On the third day, Jesus rose from the dead.
8. Crown—If we believe in Jesus, we can live with him in heaven someday.

Then have kids cut out the two scrolls, roll them up, and slip them into their Good News Shoes.

COMMITMENT

Put Your Best Foot Forward

Say: **God wants us to spread the good news. Now that you have your Good News Shoes, you'll need to decide how to use them. Turn to a partner and tell about someone you might share your Good News Shoes with this week.**

After kids have shared, say: **It's time to rap and roll! Let's learn a new verse of the "Armor of God Rap."** Review the verses that kids learned last week by having them repeat after you in a marching cadence rhythm. Then add the new verse. For extra fun, make a human train by having kids line up and hold on to the waist of the next person in line. Lead the train around the room as you say the rap:

I don't know, but I've been told
The armor of God makes me strong and *bold!*

See the helmet of salvation on my head?
God took my sins and gave me heaven instead.

Is the breastplate of righteousness on my chest?
Uh-huh! You can see that I'm wearin' God's best.

Is the belt of truth tied around my waist?
Uh-huh! I'm wrapped up in God's grace.

Is the shield of faith strapped on my arm?
Uh-huh! Satan's arrows will do me no harm.

Is the gospel of peace what I'm wearin' for shoes?
Uh-huh! And I'm ready to tell the good news.

Thank you, God, for these good gifts!
Help me live as you want me to live.

CLOSING

Gotcha Covered

Say: **Be sure to use your Good News Shoes this week, because God wants us to spread the good news.**

Have the kids take the scrolls from their Good News Shoes, and form groups of eight or fewer. Let each child pick one of the items of good news from the scrolls to thank God for. Have each group pray together.

Then gather kids in a large circle, and close with a prayer similar to this one: **Dear Lord, thank you for making us your messengers. Help us use our Good News Shoes to talk to people who need to hear about you. And please protect us with all the other pieces of armor, too. In Jesus' name, amen.**

Good News Shoes

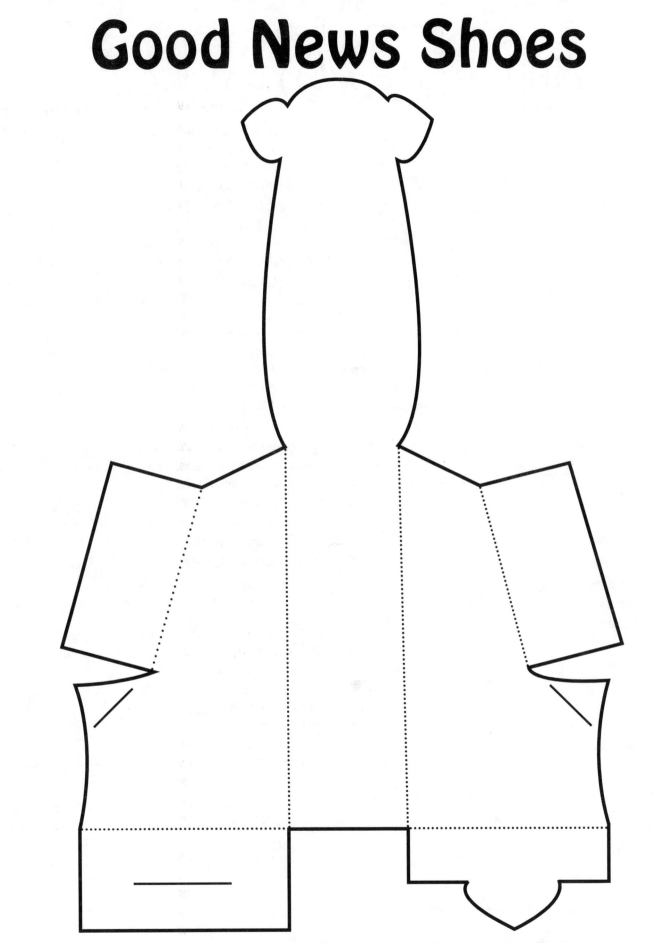

GOOD NEWS SCROLLS

"Today in the town of David a Savior has been born to you; he is Christ the Lord. This will be a sign to you: You will find a baby wrapped in cloths and lying in a manger" (Luke 2:11-12).

"Coming to his hometown, he began teaching the people in their synagogue, and they were amazed. 'Where did this man get this wisdom and these miraculous powers?' they asked. 'Isn't this the carpenter's son?' " (Matthew 13:54-55).

"Great crowds came to him, bringing the lame, the blind, the crippled, the mute and many others, and laid them at his feet; and he healed them" (Matthew 15:30).

"I am the good shepherd. The good shepherd lays down his life for the sheep" (John 10:11).

"Jesus replied, 'If anyone loves me, he will obey my teaching. My Father will love him, and we will come to him and make our home with him' " (John 14:23).

"Greater love has no one than this, that he lay down his life for his friends" (John 15:13).
    "But God demonstrates his own love for us in this: While we were still sinners, Christ died for us" (Romans 5:8).

"If you confess with your mouth, 'Jesus is Lord,' and believe in your heart that God raised him from the dead, you will be saved" (Romans 10:9).

"He humbled himself and became obedient to death—even death on a cross! Therefore God exalted him to the highest place and gave him the name that is above every name, that at the name of Jesus every knee should bow, in heaven and on earth and under the earth, and every tongue confess that Jesus Christ is Lord, to the glory of God the Father" (Philippians 2:8-11).

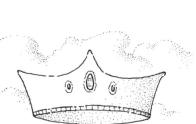

The Sword of the Spirit 4

LESSON AIM

To help kids understand that ★ God's Word makes us strong.

OBJECTIVES

Kids will
- blow paper cups over, then see that cups are stronger when they are filled with liquid;
- discover how God's Word helped Peter and John;
- learn how God's Word can make them strong today; and
- commit to wearing the armor of God.

YOU'LL NEED

- ❏ medium-size paper cups
- ❏ a watch with a second hand
- ❏ a sports drink such as Powerade or Gatorade
- ❏ Bibles
- ❏ photocopies of the "Sword of the Spirit" handout (p. 44)
- ❏ scissors

BIBLE BASIS

Acts 3:1–4:22
When Peter and John healed a well-known crippled beggar who proceeded to walk and leap around the Temple courts expressing his praise, the crowds at the Temple stood agape with wonder. Like a good preacher, Peter lost no time in proclaiming that this amazing feat had been done in the name Jesus Christ. It

was no surprise when the Temple guards escorted Peter and John to a nice, quiet cell for the remainder of the day. Early the next morning, the Sanhedrin assembled to question these "culprits" about their act of kindness to a lame man.

Did Peter and John have reason to be nervous? You bet! This was the very court that had demanded the death sentence for Jesus—and not so very long before. By all human expectations, this dynamic duo should have been drenched in perspiration. But when Peter quoted Scripture in the power of the Holy Spirit, supported by the prayers of the church, it was the members of the Sanhedrin who started to sweat! Peter and John spoke with such authority that the highest court in the land marveled at these "unschooled" men, and noted that they had been with Jesus. God's Word indeed makes us strong!

Ephesians 6:17-18

Paul finalizes his description of God's armor by admonishing us to take the sword of the Spirit. Other Scriptures pair God's Word with forceful imagery as well. Jeremiah 23:29 asks: " 'Is not my word like fire,' declares the Lord, 'and like a hammer that breaks a rock in pieces?' " Hebrews 4:12 states: "For the word of God is living and active. Sharper than any double-edged sword, it penetrates even to dividing soul and spirit, joints and marrow; it judges the thoughts and attitudes of the heart." God's Word is no benign book filled with suggestions on how to live. God's truth packs a punch that can't be ducked, sidestepped, or otherwise avoided. There's no doubting its power. It's a piece of God's armor that every Christian needs to have well in hand.

UNDERSTANDING YOUR KIDS

Many times in their lives, your kids have felt powerless. Violence and greed seem to rule the world, even in elementary school. Families separate, and children are left to contemplate what they could have done to prevent it. Nuclear and biological weapons dominate news reports and nightmares. But none of those great evils can stand before the awesome power of God's eternal, unchanging, life-giving Word. Your kids need to know that real power comes from the sword of the Spirit—and you're going to tell them this week.

The Lesson ATTENTION GRABBER

Blow Me Down!

Before class, set at least a dozen paper cups in a row along the edge of a table. As kids arrive, challenge them to estimate how many cups they can blow over or blow across the table in fifteen seconds. Let children take turns kneeling in front of the table and blowing over as many cups as they can. If time permits, let those who want to improve their scores try again.

Ask:

● **If we try this again, do you think you can blow over as many cups as you did before?**

Let each child name the number of cups he or she will blow over in the next round. Replace the cups on the edge of the table; then bring out bottles of sports drink, and fill each cup at least half full. Say: **OK, we're all set. Who wants to go first?**

Let volunteers try to blow the cups over. Of course, the liquid will weight the cups down and keep them solidly in place. After kids have tried in vain to blow the cups over, say: **After all that blowing, you're probably thirsty. Help yourself to a cup of sports drink.** Then ask:

● **How did the sports drink affect the cups?** (It made them heavier; it kept them from getting blown over.)

● **What is sports drink supposed to do for people who drink it?** (Make them stronger; give them energy.)

● **Do you believe sports drink can do all those things for you?** (Yeah, it makes me feel better; no, it doesn't really do that much.)

Say: **Sports drinks claim to make us strong. I don't know if they can really do that or not. But today we're going to learn about something that does make us strong. And it keeps us from getting blown over by difficult things that happen in life. It's the last piece of the armor of God. Actually, there are several of them in this room.**

● **Can anyone guess what I'm talking about?**

Let kids guess. If no one points out a Bible, pick up one yourself and say: **The last piece of armor is the sword of the Spirit, the Word of God. Let's get going with our Bible story and discover how God's Word makes us strong.**

TEACHER TIP

Place the cups on the forward edge of the table so that when kids blow them over, they'll remain on the table top. Have volunteer spotters stand around the table to catch any cups that roll toward the edge.

BIBLE STUDY

Trouble at the Temple (Acts 3:1–4:22)

Before class photocopy the "Trouble at the Temple" story (pp. 39-41). Cut apart the fifteen verses.

Have students form trios. If the number of kids in your class isn't divisible by three, form one group of two or four. If there are nonreaders in your class, be sure to place them with readers. Distribute the verses of the story as evenly as possible among the trios.

Say: **Decide which member of your trio will be the reader. The other two members will lead the motions. I'll give you a couple of minutes to go over your verses together.**

Have all the trios stand in one circle in the order their verses fall in the story. Explain that everyone should do the motions with the trio that's performing.

When the trios are ready, introduce the story by saying: **Our story is about two Bible heroes who got into big trouble for doing something good. But** this dynamic duo of disciples never wavered or ran away, because they knew that God's Word makes us strong.

You may want to let kids perform the story twice so they get a good grasp of the plot. At the end of the story, lead everyone in a round of applause. Then have trios scatter around the room. Ask these questions, pausing after each one to allow time for discussion.

● **How did Peter and John make the priests angry?** (They healed a man, then said they did it by faith in Jesus; they said Jesus rose from the dead.)

● **Why were Peter and John thrown in jail?** (To stop them from telling people about Jesus; to shut them up.)

● **Why was it so scary for them to be brought before the court?** (This was the same court that had put Jesus to death; members of the court were dangerous enemies of Jesus.)

● **How did Peter and John surprise the members of the court?** (They weren't scared; they were smart and strong.)

● **Why weren't Peter and John scared?** (Because they had faith in Jesus; God's Word helped them know what to say.)

● **Do you think you could be as brave as Peter and John? Explain.** (It depends; I'm not sure; I hope so.)

Say: **Peter and John stood strong in the face of pretty scary circumstances. Their strength came from knowing that they were right because they had God's Word to back them up and because they had been with Jesus.**

LIFE APPLICATION

Give Me Strength

Say: **The high court Peter and John appeared before was called the Sanhedrin. The members of the Sanhedrin tried to make life hard for the early Christians. They wanted to stop the gospel of Christ from spreading any further than it already had. What happened to Peter and John happened to lots of other Christians as well. They were arrested, threatened, thrown in jail, beaten, sometimes even killed. Jesus' enemies were sure that this kind of treatment would stomp out Christianity before it even got started.** Ask:

● **Is that what happened? Did the early Christians just cave in? Explain.** (No, they spread the good news about Jesus everywhere; no, they wouldn't give up.)

● **What gave them the strength to keep going in the face of prison and death threats?** (God's power; the Holy Spirit helped them.)

Say: **These early Christians had God's armor on. They carried the sword of the Spirit, which is the Word of God. And nothing could defeat them—not threats, not beatings, not prison, not even death!**

● **Do you know of places where Christians face those kinds of threats today?** (China; Muslim countries.)

● **When is it hard to stand strong for the Lord in our town? at your school? in your neighborhood?** (When bullies threaten me; when people use

38

Trouble at the Temple

1 Peter and John went to the Temple for prayer.
(Fold hands.)
A poor man who couldn't walk sat begging there.
(Point to one side.)
Whenever people passed him by, the beggar would say,
(Walk two fingers across your palm.)
"Alms for the poor! A few coins today?"
(Cup hands as if begging.)

2 Neither Peter nor John had money to spare,
(Hold out empty hands.)
But they had something else they were happy to share.
(Cross arms and nod head.)
Peter said, "In Jesus' name, get up and walk."
(Pretend to pull someone up.)
When the man jumped up, how people did gawk!
(Look surprised and point.)

3 The healed man jumped and leaped and praised.
(Jump and wave arms.)
The people who saw it were truly amazed!
(Look wide-eyed; cover cheeks with hands.)
"How did he do that?" everyone wondered.
(Scratch head.)
"By faith in Jesus," Peter's voice thundered.
(Point upward.)

4 Peter and John were in big trouble now.
(Shake finger.)
The priests hated Jesus, uh-huh, and how!
(Cross arms and look mean.)
"Seize them," cried a priest. "Go quickly and arrest them!
(Sweep arm to the right and point.)
Throw the culprits into jail! How we detest them!"
(Shake fists.)

5 So Peter and John spent that night in a cell,
(Pretend to hang on to bars.)
But the very next day they had a story to tell.
(Nod head.)
For early in the morning they got this command:
(Rub eyes.)
You must stand before the highest court in the land.
(Sweep arm to the left and point.)

6 That was the court that had put Jesus to death!
(Cover mouth in surprise.)
But Peter just smiled and took a deep breath.
(Smile; take a deep breath.)
A friend stood nearby on two legs that were strong—
(Stomp one foot, then the other.)
The healed man had come to right this wrong.
(Point to legs; nod.)

(continued on page 40)

7 God's Spirit filled Peter; then he began to speak.
(Raise hands, then cover heart.)
Peter felt courageous—not frightened or weak.
(Flex arm muscles.)
"This man stands before you—he used to be lame.
(Gesture to the right.)
How was he healed? By the power of Jesus' name!"
(Raise fist toward heaven.)

8 The priests all mumbled and grumbled and shuffled.
(Shake head and mumble.)
They didn't like Jesus! Their feathers were ruffled!
(Cross arms and look mean.)
Then Peter spoke again, straight from God's Word—
(Pretend to hold open Bible.)
A passage from Psalms he knew the priests had heard.
(Point to pretend Bible.)

9 "You rejected Jesus—now he's at the head.
(Point straight ahead, then up.)
You hung him on a cross, but God raised him from the dead!"
(Make cross with arms; raise hands toward heaven.)
Peter wasn't scared, though the court members raved.
(Wave arms angrily.)
He continued, "It's in Jesus' name that you must be saved!"
(Make cross with arms.)

10 The judges surely knew that their actions were wrong.
(Scratch head and look unhappy.)
Speaking from God's Word had made Peter strong.
(Pretend to hold open Bible; flex arm muscles.)
So the high priest said, "That's all we'll hear today."
(Cover ears.)
Then he called the Temple guards to take the men away.
(Walk fingers across palm.)

11 One priest said, "These men have never been to school.
(Tap head.)
How is it they can challenge us? We're the ones who rule!"
(Point thumb to chest.)
Then another said, "This is why they're so brave:
(Shake finger.)
They've been with Jesus; they said he rose from the grave."
(Make cross with arms; raise hands toward heaven.)

12 A Sadducee spoke up and asked, "What shall we do?
(Shrug shoulders.)
The whole city knows of their miracle—it's true!"
(Spread arms wide.)
"I know what to do," said another. "Let's scare them;
(Make mean face and claws.)
Say that if they preach again, we'll punish them—not spare them."
(Pretend to slap someone.)

13 When Peter and John were called back into the room,
(Walk fingers across palm.)
A loud, angry voice began to shout at them and boom.
(Cup hands around mouth.)
The angry judge warned them, "If you two want to please us,
(Shake finger.)
You'll never, never preach again in the name of Jesus."
(Shake head.)

14 Peter calmly said, "You must judge what is right:
(Point straight ahead with two fingers.)
To obey God or obey you—what's best in God's sight?
(Point toward heaven with two fingers.)
Don't even try to tell us not to say another word,
(Cover mouth and shake head.)
For we cannot stop speaking of the things we've seen and heard."
(Pull hand away; spread arms wide.)

15 There was no stopping Peter; there was no stopping John.
(Point to one side, then the other.)
God's Word made them strong—they'd preach on and on!
(Flex arm muscles.)

bad language; when people make fun of me because I'm a Christian; when teachers say the Bible isn't true.)

Say: **Let's form a circle. Now, without touching anyone, stretch your arms straight out at shoulder level, palms up, and hold that position. Good. Now while we're holding our arms like this, we'll take turns naming things that make it hard for us to stand strong for God today. It's fine to mention some of the things we just talked about. I'll begin; then we'll go around the circle to my right.**

Encourage kids to mention things such as getting teased about their faith, hearing people use God's name when they swear, being asked to cheat, being in a group that picks on people, and being invited to watch R-rated movies. After everyone has mentioned something, ask:

● **How are your arms feeling?** (Tired; sore.)

Say: **God's Word makes us strong. To feel what that's like, rest your arms on the shoulders of the people on either side of you. Doesn't that feel great? God's Word gives us that kind of help and support when we're feeling weak and discouraged. Let's find out exactly how God's Word can help us.**

COMMITMENT

Grab That Sword!

Distribute scissors and the "Sword of the Spirit" handout (p. 44).

Say: **Fold your handouts in half the long way, right down the center of the open Bible.** Pause for children to do that. **Now cut the Bible at the top from the center to the corner. Then cut at the bottom from the center to the corner.**

When kids have completed these cuts, have them open their handouts and fold up on both edges of the open Bible. Then have them fold down on the inside edges of the Bible. Demonstrate how to fold the handout into a card by folding it in half on the dotted line, then folding it closed with the Bible on the inside. When the card is opened, the Bible will pop up.

Direct kids' attention to the verse printed on the open Bible. Have a volunteer read the verse aloud, then ask:

● **Who can put that verse in their own words?** (God's Word is alive and very powerful; it helps us know what's right and wrong.)

Say: **We'll find more information about God's Word on the back of this card.** Have volunteers read the verses aloud. Then challenge kids to explain the verses in their own words. Ask:

● **What do we need to do for God's Word to be powerful and active in our lives?** (We need to read it; we need to remember what it says; we need to live the way the Bible tells us to.)

Say: **Great! And when we do those things, we allow God's Word to work in our lives, and then God's Word makes us strong.**

Rapping Up

Say: **Now we've talked about the whole armor of God. When you wear this armor, you're ready to face anything! We have one more verse to learn in our "Armor of God Rap." Here it is. Repeat after me.**

Got the sword of the Spirit, God's Holy Word?
Uh-huh! And it's full of God's power, I've heard.

Say: **Good job! Now let's do our "Armor of God Rap" one last time.**
Review the rap verses that kids have learned previously; then have fun marching in creative ways around the class as you lead the rap in a cadence rhythm:

I don't know, but I've been told
The armor of God makes me strong and _bold!_

See the helmet of salvation on my head?
God took my sins and gave me heaven instead.

Is the breastplate of righteousness on my chest?
Uh-huh! You can see that I'm wearin' God's best.

Is the belt of truth tied around my waist?
Uh-huh! I'm wrapped up in God's grace.

Is the shield of faith strapped on my arm?
Uh-huh! Satan's arrows will do me no harm.

Is the gospel of peace what I'm wearin' for shoes?
Uh-huh! And I'm ready to tell the good news.

Got the sword of the Spirit, God's Holy Word?
Uh-huh! And it's full of God's power, I've heard.

Thank you, God, for these good gifts
Help me live as you want me to live.

Say: **That was awesome! I hope you'll remember this rap, because it will remind you to take the armor of God with you wherever you go. The words are printed on the front of the cards you just made.**
And keep on studying God's Word because God's Word... (pause and let kids finish along with you) **makes us strong!**
Remind kids to take their "Sword of the Spirit" handouts as they go.

"Every word of God proves true. He defends all who come to him for protection" (Proverbs 30:5, The Living Bible).

"When you received the word of God, which you heard from us, you accepted it not as the word of men, but as it actually is, the word of God, which is at work in you who believe" (1 Thessalonians 2:13).

"For you have been born again, not of perishable seed, but of imperishable, through the living and enduring word of God. For, 'All men are like grass, and all their glory is like the flowers of the field; the grass withers and the flowers fall, but the word of the Lord stands forever.'" (1 Peter 1:23-25).

THE ARMOR OF GOD Rap

I don't know, but I've been told
The armor of God makes me strong and bold!

See the helmet of salvation on my head?
God took my sins and gave me heaven instead.

Is the breastplate of righteousness on my chest?
Uh-huh! You can see that I'm wearin' God's best.

Is the belt of truth tied around my waist?
Uh-huh! I'm wrapped up in God's grace.

Is the shield of faith strapped on my arm?
Uh-huh! Satan's arrows will do me no harm.

Is the gospel of peace what I'm wearin' for shoes?
Uh-huh! And I'm ready to tell the good news.

Got the sword of the Spirit, God's Holy Word?
Uh-huh! And it's full of God's power, I've heard.

Thank you, God, for these good gifts!
Help me live as you want me to live.

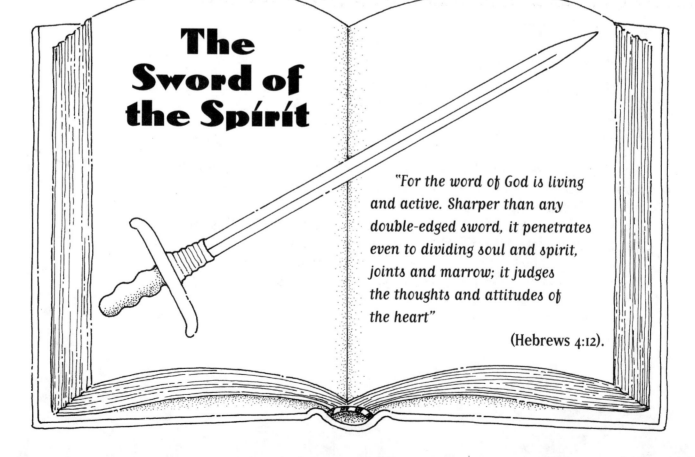

The Sword of the Spirit

"For the word of God is living and active. Sharper than any double-edged sword, it penetrates even to dividing soul and spirit, joints and marrow; it judges the thoughts and attitudes of the heart" (Hebrews 4:12).

For Everyone!

5

To help kids understand that ★ God's love is for everyone.

OBJECTIVES

Kids will
- taste various seasonings and compare them to people;
- hear how Jesus made friends with a lonely, outcast woman;
- learn that the first fruit of the Spirit is love;
- make a conversation-starter game; and
- have an opportunity to commit to showing God's love.

YOU'LL NEED

- ❑ blindfolds
- ❑ toothpicks
- ❑ paper cups
- ❑ horseradish
- ❑ honey
- ❑ vinegar
- ❑ steak sauce
- ❑ apple butter
- ❑ sour cream
- ❑ sweet and sour sauce
- ❑ orange marmalade
- ❑ a photocopy of the "Woman at the Well" pattern (p. 52) on tan paper
- ❑ a photocopy of the "Living Water" pattern (p. 53) on blue paper
- ❑ photocopies of the "Tic Tac Go-Make-a-Friend" Game Board and Game Squares (pp. 54-55)
- ❑ scissors
- ❑ pencils

BIBLE BASIS

John 4:1-42

In Jesus' time, Jewish law and rabbinical tradition firmly delineated what was appropriate social contact and what was not. Jesus calmly and purposely crossed over the line marked "appropriate" when he spoke to a Samaritan woman at a well near Sychar. Jews looked down on Samaritans to such a degree that it was typical to extend the three-day journey from Judea to Galilee to six days in order to avoid passing through Samaritan territory. With this journey through Samaria, Jesus began quietly to break down walls of prejudice and teach that God's love is for everyone. For not only was the woman Jesus spoke with a Samaritan, she was also an outcast among her own people, shunned because of her promiscuous lifestyle.

How the high and mighty Pharisees would have been shocked to see Jesus compromise his ritual cleanness by making contact with such a person! And what marvelous teaching opportunities came as a result. Because of the woman's glowing testimony and obvious transformation, Jesus and his disciples were welcomed into a village that would otherwise have been clearly hostile territory. There they remained for two days, and as Jesus preached and taught, many Samaritans came to believe in him as Savior of the world.

Galatians 5:22-23

The very first fruit of the Spirit Paul lists is love. This is not surprising at all, because when we allow God's Spirit to transform our minds and hearts, God's love begins to flow from an eternal, unstoppable river. Before long, it overflows—we can't help it! We can resist, by clinging stubbornly to sinful attitudes. But when we totally submit ourselves to the Spirit's power, there's no avoiding it—we have to go with the flow! This great outpouring of love isn't meant to sprinkle just a chosen few family members and church friends; it's meant to go splashing and swirling around every person we touch until our world is awash with the glow of it!

UNDERSTANDING YOUR KIDS

Children tend to develop the majority of their relationships within certain comfort zones. Typically, kids' comfort zones form along lines similar to their parents'. Unfortunately, many Christian families choose to remain within the confines of a safe circle of Christian friends, seldom cultivating friendships among those who don't know Christ. If parents tend to restrict their associations to friends of their own religious community and socioeconomic class, chances are their children will do the same.

While it may be difficult for adults to learn to break those patterns, it's easy enough for children. Use this lesson to teach kids how to reach out to children who are different, lonely, and lacking in friends, to show them that God's love is for everyone.

Taste Test

Before kids arrive, set out blindfolds, toothpicks, and paper cups containing small amounts of each of the following items: horseradish, honey, vinegar, steak sauce, apple butter, sour cream, sweet and sour sauce, and orange marmalade. Cover the cups so kids can't see their contents, and set the cups around the room. Place toothpicks by each cup.

As kids arrive, help them form pairs. Let each pair decide which partner will be blindfolded.

Say: **If you're not wearing a blindfold, lead your partner to one of the cups you see around the room. Dip a toothpick into the cup, and give it to your partner to taste. Blindfolded partners, when you taste what's on your toothpick, finish this sentence: "This reminds me of a person who is..." Then think of a person who's like that, but don't say the person's name out loud. Once you've thought of someone, say to your partner, "Next!" Then you'll go on to another taste test. When you've tasted what's in all eight cups, switch roles with your partner.**

As kids move around the room tasting what's in the various cups, remind them what to say and what to think about. After everyone has completed the taste test, collect the blindfolds, throw away the toothpicks, and gather kids in a circle. Ask:

● **What makes some people happy and others crabby?** (The things that happen to them; the choices they make.)

● **Did you ever know someone who absolutely everyone liked? What made that person so likable?** (She was always nice; he seemed to care about everyone.)

● **Did you ever know someone who absolutely no one liked? What was so unlikable about that person?** (No matter how nice I tried to be to her, she was always nasty; he acted as if he was better than everyone.)

● **Did you ever have a day when you felt unlikable—when nearly everyone was fed up with you? What was that like?** (I got in a really bad mood, and I just couldn't get out of it; I took everything the wrong way; I wanted to be nicer, but I just couldn't do it.)

Say: **Nearly all of us have days when we're more like horseradish or vinegar than honey. And that feels pretty bad—even for just one day. But suppose you felt like that for weeks or months or even years. Yuck! The person we're going to hear about in today's Bible story was a horseradish person, and she probably had been like that for a long time. Fortunately, she ran into someone who knew that God's love is for everyone.**

Jesus Makes a Friend (John 4:1-42)

Before class, photocopy the "Woman at the Well" pattern (p. 52) onto tan paper. Photocopy the "Living Water" pattern (p. 53) onto blue paper. During the story, you'll want to hold the printed sides of the patterns so they face the children. You may want to color the well scene to add visual interest.

Say: **One day, Jesus and his disciples traveled to the town of Sychar (SIGH-kar). It was unusual for Jews to travel to Sychar because Samaritans lived there, and Jews and Samaritans didn't get along. In fact, they usually avoided each other, even if it meant traveling miles out of their way. But Jesus didn't mind passing through Samaritan country.**

Fold the tan paper back on Line 1 so only the well shows.

Jesus' disciples went into town to find something to eat while Jesus rested by a well on the outskirts of town. Before long, a woman came to the well to draw water.

Open the paper at Line 1, and fold it back at Line 2 so the well and one person are showing.

It was strange for anyone to come to the well at noon when it was hot. The big jars of water were heavy to carry, so most people came to the well when it was cooler. Jesus knew that this woman had come to the well alone because nobody liked her. Other women enjoyed meeting their friends at the well, but this woman had no friends to meet.

Cut the paper from A to B. Open the figure on Line 2 so both people show.

"Give me a drink," Jesus said.

The woman was shocked. Who was this Jewish man who dared talk to her?

"How is it that you, a Jewish man, are asking for a drink from me, a Samaritan woman?" she asked him.

Jesus replied, "If you knew about God's free gift and if you knew who I was, you'd be asking me, and I'd give you living water."

Fold the blue paper in half on Line 1.

Now that left the woman feeling a little confused!

"You have no bucket, and this well is deep," she said. "Where does your living water come from?"

Cut the paper from A to B. Fold down on Line 2, and display the jar.

Jesus gave her another confusing answer. "Everyone who drinks this water will be thirsty again, but whoever drinks the living water I give...

Open the fold on Line 2, and cut from B to C.

will never be thirsty again. The water I give will become a well of water within him...

Tip the jar and "pour" the stream of water.

springing up to eternal life."

Now Jesus really had the woman's attention!

"Sir," she said, "give me this water!"

Jesus replied, "First, go and bring your husband."

The woman was embarrassed. "I have no husband," she answered.

48

"You're right," he said. "You've had five husbands, and you're not married to the man you're living with now."

The woman could hardly believe her ears. This stranger knew all about her! He knew why she had no friends—no one wanted to be friends with a woman who had such a bad reputation. The woman realized that Jesus must be someone special.

"I know that God is sending the Messiah," she said. "The Messiah will tell us all about God."

Jesus said, "I am the Messiah."

The woman gasped. Could it be true? She got so excited that she left her water jar and went running back into town. "Come see this man I talked to," she told the townspeople. "He knew all about me! Do you think he could be the Messiah God promised to send?"

A crowd of people followed the woman back to the well to meet Jesus. They begged him to stay in their town and teach. So Jesus stayed two more days, and many people believed that he was the Savior God had promised.

Ask:

● **How did Jesus make friends with the woman at the well?** (He asked her for a drink; he spoke to her, even though she didn't expect him to.)

● **Was Jesus expected to make friends with her? Explain.** (No, because Jews and Samaritans didn't like each other; no, men and women who were strangers to each other didn't speak to each other without a reason.)

● **Why did he bother to make friends with her?** (He knew she was lonely, and he cared about her; he knew he could help her.)

● **What good things happened because Jesus took time to make friends with this woman?** (She believed in him, and so did lots of her neighbors; a whole town got to hear Jesus and believe in him.)

Say: **Jesus came to show us that God's love is for everyone. He was ready and willing to offer his friendship to a total stranger. But he became much more than her friend—he became her Savior.**

LIFE APPLICATION

Tic Tac Go-Make-a-Friend!

Ask:

● **When the people of Sychar looked at the woman Jesus met, what did they see?** (Someone with a bad reputation; someone they wanted to avoid.)

● **When Jesus looked at the woman, what did he see?** (Someone who was lonely; someone who needed to be forgiven of her sins.)

● **Do you suppose the woman was friendly to the people of Sychar? Why or why not?** (No, because they avoided her; no, because they were unfriendly to her.)

● **Which of the seasonings you sampled earlier do you think best represents this woman?**

Say: **One of the amazing things about Jesus was that he knew how to** make friends with people—how to approach people who were hurting without scaring them or looking down on them or driving them away. His first act of friendship was simply to ask for a drink of water. Ask:

● **Have you ever made friends with someone who was unfriendly at first and hard to get to know? What was that like?** (I had to keep being friendly to her for a long time before she started being friendly to me; I kept smiling at him and trying to think of nice things to say.)

Say: **It's easy to make friends with people who are cheerful and outgoing. But vinegar/horseradish people are another matter—they can be quite a challenge. God's love is for everyone, including horseradish people. Jesus showed us by his example with the woman at the well that people who are hard to get to know need God's love just as much as everyone else. But making friends with them might seem a little risky.**

Let's have some fun making a game called Tic Tac Go-Make-a-Friend. The game will help us learn how to reach out and make friends with people, even those who might be a bit difficult to get to know.

Distribute scissors and photocopies of the "Tic Tac Go-Make-a-Friend" handouts (pp. 54-55). Show kids how to cut apart the game squares, then fold the game board page into an envelope, and drop the game squares inside. Have kids write their names on the outside of their envelopes. Distribute pencils and say: **Once you've finished making your game, find a partner—preferably someone you don't know very well. Arrange the game squares in any order on the game board. Play the game just as you would Tick-Tack-Toe. When you lift a game square, answer the question or do what the card says; then lightly mark your initial in that square on the game board. Try to get four squares in a row in any direction.**

Let kids play two or three rounds of the game with different partners if time allows.

COMMITMENT

The First Fruit

Call time and bring everyone together. Ask:

● **When and where could you use this game to reach out and make a new friend?** (On the playground; at recess; with my new neighbor.)

● **Why would you _want_ to reach out to someone who's not very friendly?** (To show God's love; so I could eventually tell that person about Jesus.)

Say: **During this lesson we've learned that God's love is for everyone. Love is the first item on a list the Bible calls "the fruit of the Spirit." Listen carefully as I read about the fruit of the Spirit from Galatians 5:22-23. See if you can tell me how many fruits there are.** Read Galatians 5:22-23 aloud. Ask:

● **How many fruits are there?** (Nine.)

Say: **It's important to understand that these things come from God's Holy Spirit. When we open our lives to God and invite his Holy Spirit to work in our hearts, God puts these things in our lives. Right now I have** a great song that will help you remember the fruit of the Spirit in a really unique way.

Teach kids this song to the tune of "Rock Around the Clock."

The Fruit of the Spirit
(to the tune of "Rock Around the Clock")

Love and joy.
Love, joy, peace.
In your heart may they increase.
We're talking patience, kindness, goodness, too.
And faithfulness to last your whole life through.
Gentleness and self-control—
The fruit God's Spirit grows in you!
(Repeat)

Say: **Good job! Keep singing that song this week, and you'll know what to be watching for as God helps you grow.**

CLOSING

Open Hearts

Show kids how to make a heart with their hands by bending their fingers, touching the fingernails and heel of one hand to the other. The space between their hands will be the shape of a heart. Say: **Let's end today by opening our hearts to God and asking the Holy Spirit to be at work in our lives.** As you speak, turn your hands so that the palms are facing upward, and straighten your fingers to "open" the heart. **As we pray, I'd like you to close your eyes so that you don't see what others are doing. If you'd like to make a commitment to God to show his love to others this week, make that heart with your hands, and open it in the same way we just did as I pray.**

Pray: **Dear Lord, thank you for showing us that God's love is for everyone. Please help us this week as we look for ways to reach out to people who seem unfriendly and unhappy. Lord, we open our hearts to you. We ask your Holy Spirit to work in our lives and bring forth the fruit of love. In Jesus' name, amen.**

Remind kids to take their games. Encourage them to use the game to reach out in love and make a new friend this week.

The Woman at the Well

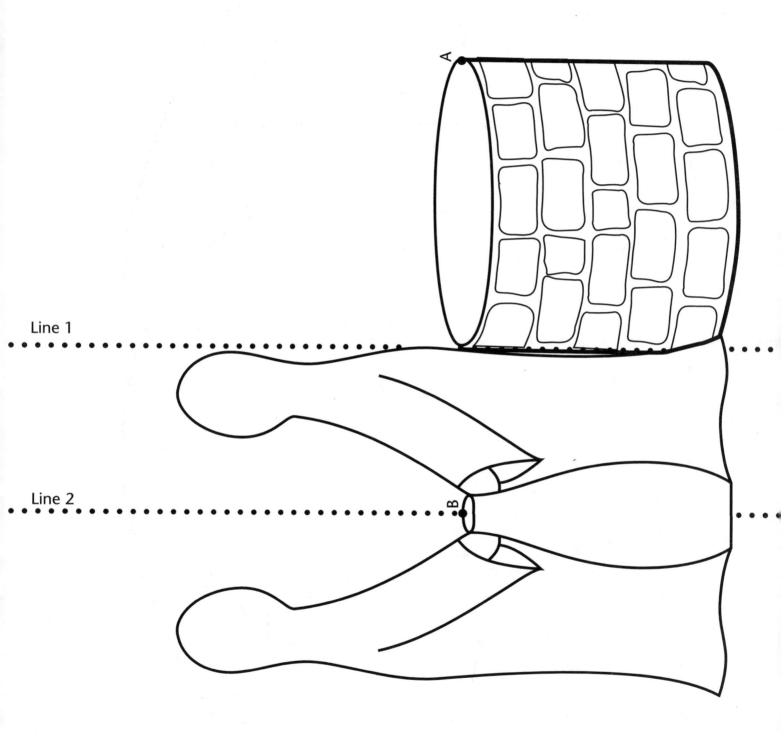

Line 1

Line 2

Living Water

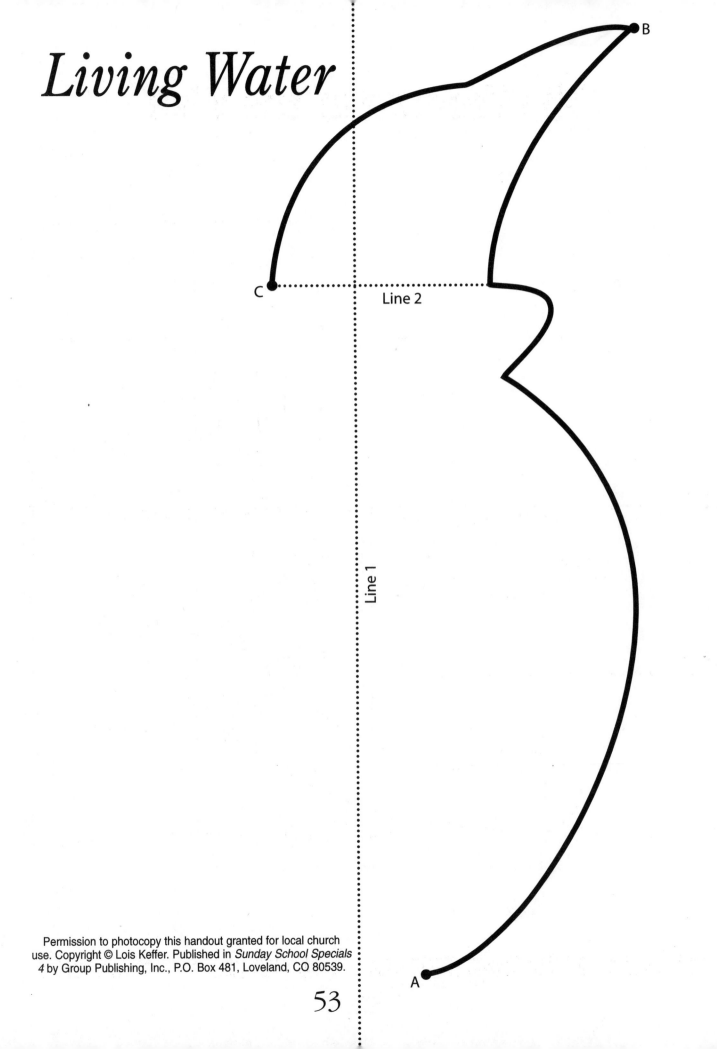

C .... Line 2

Line 1

Tic Tac Go-Make-A-Friend

Play this game like Tick-Tack-Toe. To claim a square, lift the game piece, do what it says, then write your initial lightly on the game board. The first person to get four squares in a row in any direction wins.

1. Fold the game board in thirds horizontally on the dotted lines.

2. Make two more folds on the vertical dotted lines.

3. Fold the left end into a point.

4. Turn both ends toward the center. Tuck the point into the right end to make a handy envelope in which to store your game squares.

Tic Tac Go-Make-A-Friend
Game Squares

If you could go anywhere at all for a vacation, where would you go?	Sing two lines of your favorite song.	Who's your favorite relative? What do you like about that person?	Tell about a time you were really, really happy.
Name three games you like to play.	What's your all-time favorite movie?	What's your middle name?	Tell what you know about who Jesus is.
Who's your favorite singer? your favorite group?	What do you think you'd like to do when you grow up?	What was your best-ever birthday present?	What's your favorite food?
Tell about a time you were really, really sad.	If you could meet anyone who's ever lived, who would you want to meet?	What's your favorite sports team?	When has God answered a prayer for you?

6 Paul and Silas, Partners in Joy

LESSON AIM

To help kids understand that ★ God gives us joy in good times and bad.

OBJECTIVES

Kids will
- play a game to experience the ups and downs of life,
- learn how Paul and Silas sang hymns of praise in prison,
- discover how to find joy in the midst of difficult circumstances, and
- have an opportunity to make a commitment to be joyful.

YOU'LL NEED

- ❏ used office paper
- ❏ markers
- ❏ masking tape
- ❏ photocopies of the "Game of Life" handout (p. 65)
- ❏ a basket
- ❏ red and blue baseball caps
- ❏ red and blue markers
- ❏ photocopies of the "Joy Box" handout (p. 66)
- ❏ scissors
- ❏ glue sticks
- ❏ pencils, erasers, or clean stones
- ❏ an X-Acto knife

Acts 16:16-40

Paul and Silas turned their missionary efforts toward the Greek city of Philippi. As they preached and taught in that city, they were bothered by a demon-possessed slave girl who for many days followed them shouting, "These men are servants of the Most High God who are telling you the way to be saved." While at first glance her proclamation might seem to have been positive, in fact the "Most High God" was just one of many gods of pagan religion. Even if she were referring to the one true and eternal God, her presence became such a distraction that Paul finally cast the demon out of her. This infuriated her owners, who had been making *their* fortune from *her* ability to tell fortunes. Freed of the demon, the girl lost her "fortunetelling" abilities, and her owners lost their income.

What happened next was not pretty. The owners had Paul and Silas dragged before city officials, accusing them of causing an uproar against mandated emperor worship. They were stripped, beaten, and thrown in jail.

It would be miserable enough to be humiliated, beaten, and jailed for doing something bad. But to have imprisonment set in motion by setting a slave girl free from a demonic spirit? Now there's cause for complaint. In the inner darkness of a foul, dank Philippian prison, did anyone hear Paul and Silas complaining? No—they heard the duo singing hymns of praise! Their midnight melodies caught the ears of the other prisoners, and before the night was over, God's love had captured the jailer's heart.

The joy that the Holy Spirit gives is not dependent on outward circumstances. It springs from knowing that God is in control, that our trust in him will always be rewarded, and that the ultimate victory is ours. Such joy cannot be altered or extinguished, and it's more contagious than the measles!

Galatians 5:22

According to the NIV Exhaustive Concordance, the word "joy" or its derivative appears in Scripture more than 250 times. Now that's a recurring theme! Paul made joy second on his list of fruits of the Spirit. The Spirit works in us to guide our hearts and minds toward things we have to be thankful for, rather than allowing us to focus on pain and disappointment. Most of us are drawn to joyful people. Anyone can be happy when things are going right. It's those whose joy shines through adversity who truly light the path to God.

UNDERSTANDING YOUR KIDS

This media generation lives with certain basic misconceptions about life that are generated and perpetuated by television dramas and sitcoms. Those misconceptions can be boiled down to something along these lines: We should all be beautiful, healthy, slender, and well-toned; we should live in comfortable, well-appointed homes; and we should have enough money to dress stylishly and pursue a variety of leisure-time activities. These external things are supposed to equal happiness. Because this image is portrayed by so much of U.S. television, many people around the world who view the programs in syndication tend to think of Americans in these terms. No wonder our own children pick up on these ideas!

As children approach the middle grades, they begin to distinguish between joy, which springs from trust in God's never-failing love and care, and happiness, which depends on feelings. Use this lesson to teach kids that one of the distinguishing characteristics of a Christian's life is joy that does not waver when it's tested by difficult circumstances.

The Lesson ATTENTION GRABBER

The Game of Life

Before class, lay twenty-five sheets of used office paper on the floor in a curving game path. Write "Start" on the first sheet and "Finish" on the last one. You may want to secure the papers lightly with a small strip of masking tape. Cut apart the strips on the "Game of Life" handout (p. 65), and place them in a basket.

When the first child arrives, mark his or her hand with the red marker. Mark the hand of the next child with the blue marker. Continue alternating colors until all the children have arrived. (Don't worry about having even numbers of older and younger children on these teams.) Have the teams line up near Start. Put the red baseball cap on the first player of the red team and the blue baseball cap on the first player of the blue team. Have both players stand with one foot on Start.

Say: **Welcome to The Game of Life. We're going to let representatives of each team take turns drawing slips of paper from the basket. When it's your turn, you'll read the slip aloud, then go forward or back the number of spaces it says. If you're told to go back and you're still at Start, you'll just stay at Start until a player gets a slip that says to move forward. The first team to reach Finish wins. Ready? Here we go.**

Have both players draw slips, read them aloud, and move forward the appropriate number of spaces or remain at Start. Then have the next two players replace the first two on the game path, put on the caps, draw and read their slips, and move along the game path accordingly. Keep rotating players and passing the caps from team member to team member. Have players hang on to their slips as the game progresses. Play until one team reaches Finish.

Then collect the caps and slips, gather everyone in a circle, and ask:
- **Did you think this game was very much like real life? Why or why not?** (Yes, because I couldn't tell what was going to happen next; no, because things don't happen so fast in real life.)
- **What's it like when you get a lot of "go back" slips and can't ever seem to move forward?** (Really discouraging; it makes me want to quit.)
- **How is that like what sometimes happens in real life?** (Sometimes

TEACHER TIP

If no one reaches Finish by the time you've used all the slips, collect the slips, put them back in the basket, and reuse them. At the end of five minutes, declare the winner to be the team that's closest to Finish.

58

a lot of bad things happen right in a row; sometimes things seem to go from bad to worse.)

● **What can you tell us about a time like that in your life?** (My dad got sick and couldn't work, and right after that our car broke down; my parents separated, and I started getting really bad grades in school.)

● **Share a time in your life when a whole lot of good things happened.** (My brother came home from the Army just in time for my birthday last year, and my sister won the city spelling bee; my mom got well from cancer and got to go back to work.)

Say: **When you drew a slip out of the basket, you didn't know if it would bring something happy or sad. Each new day is kind of like that—we just don't know what it will bring. But today we're going to learn that God gives us joy in good times and bad. And we're going to learn it from some guys who knew what it's like to have a *really* bad day.**

BIBLE STUDY

Paul and Silas (Acts 16:16-40)

Say: **Our story is about two missionaries named Paul and Silas. It took place a few years after Jesus went back to heaven. At the beginning of the story, any time you want to, you may call out, "Hey, you!" But after I say the word "out," there'll be no more "Hey, you's"—you'll just listen quietly and wait for my next directions. Got that?** Ask:

● **When will you call out, "Hey, you!"?** (At the beginning of the story.)

● **When will you listen quietly and wait for my next directions?** (When you say "out.")

Say: **Good. Here we go.**

Ignore kids as they call out, "Hey, you!" Just calmly tell the story.

Say: **Paul and Silas traveled together wherever God guided them. They preached and taught about Jesus as they went from town to town. In Philippi they stayed at the home of a wealthy merchant named Lydia who had come to believe in Jesus.**

One day Paul and Silas and some of their friends were on their way through town when they met a slave girl who was controlled by an evil spirit. Whenever she saw Paul and Silas, she cried, "These men are servants of the Most High God, who are telling you the way to be saved." Days went by, and each time the slave girl saw Paul and Silas, she would shout after them, just as you're yelling to me and interrupting me right now. Now the owners of this slave girl were greedy men. Because of the evil spirit, the girl was able to tell fortunes. So her owners made a lot of money from people paying to have the girl tell their fortunes. They didn't care one bit about how unhappy and frightened the girl was.

One day when the girl was following Paul and Silas and shouting to them, Paul decided that he'd had enough. He turned and said to the evil spirit, "In the name of Jesus Christ I command you to come *out* of her." Immediately the evil spirit left the girl, and she stopped calling out, just

as you've stopped calling out to me.

If the slave girl's owners had been kind and compassionate, they would have been glad for her. Instead, all they could think about was the money that they would no longer make since she couldn't tell fortunes anymore. These greedy men were so angry that they turned the crowd against Paul and Silas. The owners dragged the two missionaries to the marketplace and brought them before the authorities. Without any kind of fair trial at all, the magistrates had Paul and Silas stripped and severely beaten, then hauled off to prison.

"Guard these men carefully," the leaders ordered the jailer. So the jailer threw the bruised and bleeding missionaries into the dark inner room of the prison and locked their feet in heavy wooden stocks.

Let's see what that might have been like. I'd like you to move and form a large circle with a couple of feet of space between each person.

Scatter pencils, erasers, or clean stones on the floor in the spaces between the children. Don't join the circle yourself.

Then say: **Now turn and lie down so your feet are near, but not touching, the head of the person next to you. Don't move any of the things on the floor—just lie down right on top of them.** Help children arrange themselves head-to-toe on the floor. When everyone is in place, say: **Good. It wasn't very comfortable sleeping on the floor in prison. Now to imagine what it might have been like for Paul and Silas to have their feet in stocks, I'd like you to reach up behind your head and grasp the ankles of the person behind you. Grasp them firmly, but don't squeeze hard.** Help children grasp each other's ankles. Make sure no one is being rough.

Say: **Now let me remind you that the prison was dark, damp, and smelly.** Ask:

● **How do you think Paul and Silas were feeling?** (Lousy; worse than I am right now.)

Say: **You know, if I were in that situation, I might be wishing for a really kind, gentle doctor or nurse to wash my wounds with warm water, to dress them with some kind of soothing ointment, and to give me some medicine to help the pain. I'd probably think of a soft, warm bed with a warm quilt, and maybe a nice goose-feather pillow. Do you think Paul and Silas might have been wishing for those things?**

Well, they weren't. In fact, they were thinking of something quite different, and all the other prisoners knew it. Do you know how they knew it? Because a strange sound started coming from that inner cell. It was the sound of singing! In that dark, stinking cell, bruised and bloody as they were, Paul and Silas started singing hymns of praise to God.

Maybe you'd like to sing a little song with me to show how happy you are right now. Let's sing "I've Got the Joy."

If your kids are unfamiliar with this song, teach them these simple lyrics:

I've got the joy, joy, joy, joy down in my heart!
Down in my heart, down in my heart.
I've got the joy, joy, joy, joy down in my heart,
Down in my heart to stay!

Say: **Well, that wasn't exactly the best singing you've ever done, but I**

60

can forgive you, considering the circumstances. Why don't you sit up and get comfortable now?

It was precisely the miserable circumstances that made Paul and Silas' joyful hymns of praise so remarkable. And the other prisoners took notice. Paul and Silas taught them—and the jailer—the unforgettable lesson that God gives us joy in good times and bad. Ask:

● **What reasons did Paul and Silas have for not being joyful?** (They'd been beaten and embarrassed in public; they'd been sent to prison without a trial; they were injured and in pain; all this had happened because they'd done something good.)

Say: **The joy that Paul and Silas felt wasn't humanly possible. From a human standpoint, they should have been feeling wretched and angry. Their joy came from the Holy Spirit. When Paul later wrote about the fruit of the Spirit, he listed joy second, just after love.** Ask:

● **What thoughts do you think inspired Paul and Silas to sing hymns of praise in the middle of the night loudly enough to be heard by the other prisoners?** (God had a plan; they were glad to be serving God, and that was more important to them than anything else.)

Say: **We can never really know what Paul and Silas were thinking, but based on letters Paul wrote that are in the Bible, we can imagine. He believed it was a privilege to suffer for the cause of Christ. He was thankful for the young church that was starting in Philippi. And Paul believed that "in all things God works for the good of those who love him, who have been called according to his purpose." That's found in Romans 8:28. It's that attitude that makes God-given joy different from happiness. When we believe that God is in control and is working for our good in everything that happens, the Holy Spirit gives us joy that nothing can take away.**

That's just the beginning of what happened that night. God sent an earthquake that shook loose all the chains and opened the doors of the prison. Thinking that all his prisoners would escape, the jailer was about to commit suicide. But Paul stopped him and reassured him that everyone was still there. The jailer fell before Paul and asked, "What must I do to be saved?" That night, the jailer and his whole family became Christians, and their entire household was filled with joy.

LIFE APPLICATION

Joy in Tough Times

Ask:

● **Do you think God can still give people that kind of joy today? Why or why not?** (Yes, because I've seen people who are still joyful when bad things happen to them; no, nobody can be happy when things are that bad.)

Say: **I'm going to share with you three brief, true stories of people who experienced the worst kinds of discouragement. I'll tell each story in two parts. Between the two sections of each story, I'll give you a** chance to tell me how that person might find joy. So listen carefully.

"It was so difficult when my husband died," said Darlene, a middle-aged woman. "Taking care of him was a full-time job. I hadn't worked for so long that we were terribly in debt. There was no way I could make my house payments. And I needed a car."

Ask:

● **Do you see any way Darlene could find joy in this situation? Why or why not?** (No, because she lost her husband and she might lose her house; yes, because you never know what God might do.)

Say: **Let's hear the rest of Darlene's story.**

"The people at church were so amazing. They made my house payments for three months. And one Sunday someone just came up to me and handed me the keys to a car and said, 'It's yours.' It was just one miracle after another. God kept all his promises."

Say: **Here's the next story.**

"Grandma Jones lives in terrible pain all the time," the pastor told his family. "An operation could help a lot, but her heart is too weak. The operation could kill her. So her doctor tells her she just has to live with the pain."

Ask:

● **Do you think there's any way Grandma Jones could be a joyful person? Explain.** (No, not if she hurt all the time; maybe, if they gave her medicine to help her pain.)

Say: **Here's what else the pastor told his family.**

"But every time I leave the nursing home after visiting her, I feel so full of joy. Her face is always aglow with smiles. She looks forward to heaven so much—it's all she thinks about. I go in there to cheer her up, but she ends up cheering me up! Heaven is so real to her. Visiting her makes me look forward to heaven, too."

Say: **Remember, these are based on true stories. And I have one more for you.**

"When my dad lost his job, our family hardly knew what to do," Brenda explained. "Then my mom got a job offer in another state. None of us wanted to move away from our home, our church, and our friends. We all cried when the 'For Sale' sign went up in front of our house."

Ask:

● **How do you think Brenda's family could find joy?** (They might not have to move after all; something really good might happen in their new town.)

Here is what Brenda said happened: "Less than a month after our move, Dad was hired at the same company where Mom was working. It was the kind of job he'd always dreamed of. It turned out that Dad losing his old job was the best thing that could have happened."

Ask:

● **What did the people in these three stories have in common?** (They were all hurting; terrible things happened to them.)

● **How could they find joy in their difficult situations?** (They trusted that God would take care of them; they kept believing that God would help them, and God did.)

● **How were the people in these stories like Paul and Silas?** (They all found joy even when things were terrible.)

Say: **All these people found out that God gives us joy in good times and bad. The way we learn to hang on to joy in bad times is to realize how much God loves us and cares for us. Let's have fun making little "Joy Box" jukeboxes that will remind us to rely on God's care in tough times.**

COMMITMENT

Joy to Go!

Before class, prepare the "Joy Box" handouts (p. 66) by using an X-Acto knife to open the slits between the two sets of dots on the front of the jukebox.

Distribute the "Joy Box" handouts (p. 66). Show kids how to cut off the strip of verses, then cut out the jukebox on the heavy lines. Make mountain folds on the dotted lines, and fold the sides down around the front to create a jukebox shape. Have kids rub a glue stick on tabs A and B and secure the tabs behind the front of the jukebox as shown on the handout.

Demonstrate how to slip the strip of verses through the slits so the verses are displayed on the front of the jukebox. Then have kids tape the ends of the verse strip together to form a loop.

As kids are cutting and assembling their Joy Boxes, mingle and discuss the following questions:

● **How could your Joy Box encourage you when you're going through a difficult time?** (I could read the verses and remember that God cares for me; the verses could remind me to trust God no matter what.)

● **How could you use it to encourage someone who seems to have no hope or joy at all?** (I could share it with them; I could tell them about Paul and Silas and read them the verses.)

● **What is the secret to having joy in good times and bad?** (To trust God; to remember that God loves me and that he is in control and will take care of me.)

Say: **When we truly trust God and realize how very much God loves us and wants the best for us, God gives us joy that nothing can take away. That doesn't mean that all of our moments will be happy ones. But we can trust in God's love and care for us. That's how God gives us joy in good times and bad.**

CLOSING

Sing It Out!

Say: **As I mentioned earlier, joy is second in Paul's list of the fruit of the Spirit.** Ask:

● **What are some other things on the list?**

Say: **I guess after today's story, we've learned that Paul knew what he** was talking about. The same man who sang when he was beaten and bloody in prison is the man who wrote this list. So let's sing out for Paul.

As you teach kids the following song, you may want to have them follow along in their Bibles.

The Fruit of the Spirit
(to the tune of "Rock Around the Clock")

Love and joy.
Love, joy, peace.
In your heart may they increase.
We're talking patience, kindness, goodness, too.
And faithfulness to last your whole life through.
Gentleness and self-control—
The fruit God's Spirit grows in you!
(Repeat)

Say: **I hope you'll let the Holy Spirit work in your heart so all these wonderful things will become part of you. This week, remember that God gives us joy in good times and bad. No matter what happens, hang on to that joy!**

Remind kids to take their Joy Boxes with them as they leave.

The Game of Life

Cut apart the slips, and place them in a basket.

Your mom got a promotion at work. Move ahead 2 spaces.	A storm took the roof off your house. Go back 3 spaces.	Your best friend had to move to a different state. Go back 3 spaces.
Your family won a magazine sweepstakes. Move ahead 5 spaces.	You won the citywide spelling bee. Move ahead 3 spaces.	Your dad's job was cut, and he's looking for work. Go back 3 spaces.
You got a great report card. Move ahead 2 spaces.	You broke your ankle and have to miss the whole soccer season. Go back 2 spaces.	Your neighbor's house was robbed, and you're afraid the same thing might happen to you. Go back 1 space.
Your family got the new car you wanted. Move ahead 1 space.	Your favorite team won the World Series. Move ahead 1 space.	You didn't come home on time and got grounded for a week. Go back 1 space.
Your favorite uncle is coming to visit. Move ahead 1 space.	It's Christmas! Move ahead 3 spaces.	You got a raise in your allowance. Move ahead 1 space.
You got a new puppy. Move ahead 1 space.	Your fish died. Go back 1 space.	It's your birthday! Move ahead 2 spaces.
You had your tonsils out. Go back 3 spaces.	You didn't get the part you wanted in the school play. Go back 1 space.	You get to go to Walt Disney World for vacation. Move ahead 3 spaces.
You made a new friend. Move ahead 1 space.	You lost your tickets to an NBA game. Go back 1 space.	The neighborhood kids are mad at you. Go back 1 space.

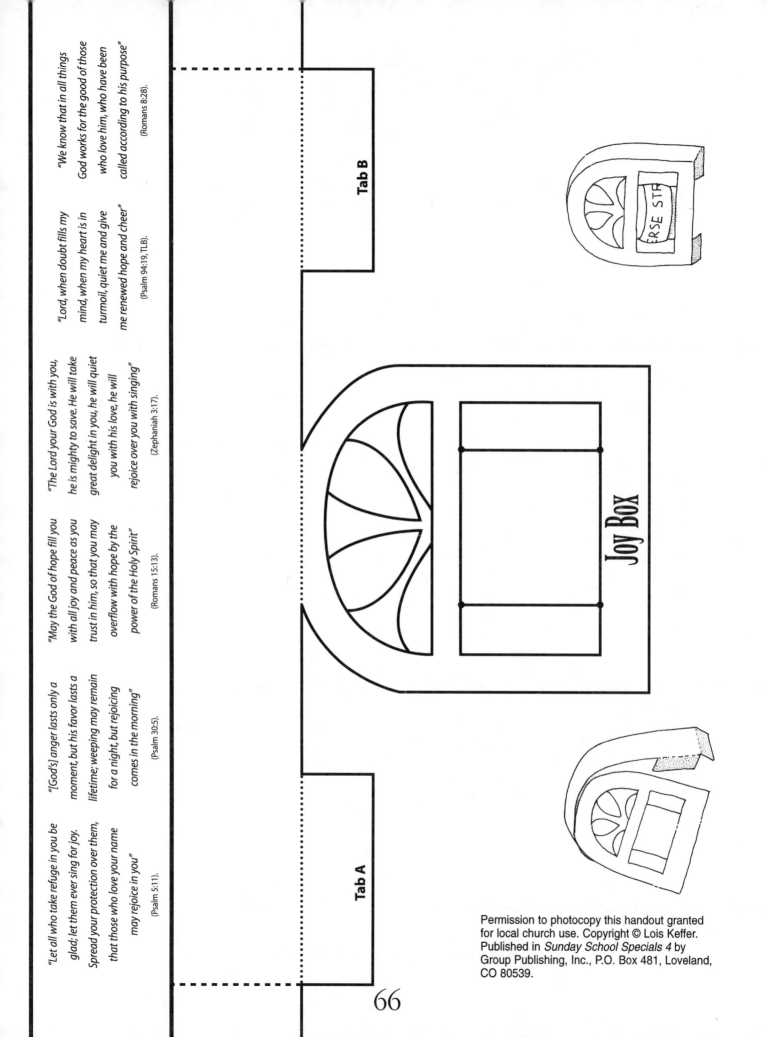

"Let all who take refuge in you be glad; let them ever sing for joy. Spread your protection over them, that those who love your name may rejoice in you" (Psalm 5:11).

"[God's] anger lasts only a moment, but his favor lasts a lifetime; weeping may remain for a night, but rejoicing comes in the morning" (Psalm 30:5).

"May the God of hope fill you with all joy and peace as you trust in him, so that you may overflow with hope by the power of the Holy Spirit" (Romans 15:13).

"The Lord your God is with you, he is mighty to save. He will take great delight in you, he will quiet you with his love, he will rejoice over you with singing" (Zephaniah 3:17).

"Lord, when doubt fills my mind, when my heart is in turmoil, quiet me and give me renewed hope and cheer" (Psalm 94:19, TLB).

"We know that in all things God works for the good of those who love him, who have been called according to his purpose" (Romans 8:28).

Tab B

Tab A

Joy Box

A Tale of Two Sisters

7

LESSON AIM

To help kids understand that ★ God wants us to be at peace.

OBJECTIVES

Kids will
- have fun getting all worked up, then learn how to be at peace;
- hear how Martha got all worked up while Mary sat peacefully at Jesus' feet;
- learn the value of being at peace;
- make a craft that teaches them how to spend peaceful moments with Jesus; and
- have an opportunity to commit to spending time with Jesus each day.

YOU'LL NEED

- ❑ bubble gum
- ❑ a CD player
- ❑ a CD of ocean surf or peaceful worship music
- ❑ photocopies of the "Tale of Two Sisters" story (pp. 71-72)
- ❑ two scarves (optional)
- ❑ photocopies of the "Pocketful of Peace" handout (p. 76)
- ❑ an X-Acto knife
- ❑ scissors

BIBLE BASIS

Luke 10:38-42
Jesus was evidently a frequent and welcome visitor at the Bethany home of

Mary, Martha, and Lazarus. Imagine the flurry of activity the Lord's visits must have caused, for he brought with him his disciples and any number of extraneous followers. All these folks needed to be fed and given beds at night. Hospitality was given without reservation—but not without a fair amount of wear and tear.

Martha stomped grim-faced through the house seeing to all the important things that occupy a competent hostess as Mary sat serenely at Jesus' feet, drinking in his teaching, reveling in his presence. Can you see Martha wiping a trickle of sweat, tucking back a stray hair, then letting out a deep sigh of frustration as she approached Jesus with her complaint about her unhelpful sister? How she must have cringed at Jesus' rebuke. And to be caught by a gospel writer who recorded her faux pas for generations of Christians to learn from! Aren't you glad it wasn't *you?* (And couldn't it well have been you, any number of times in your life?)

Who could blame Martha, after all? Wasn't she seeing to everyone's needs, serving as Christ taught us to serve? Yes, but Jesus very clearly placed the higher value on Mary's single-minded devotion to him. Jesus commended the peaceful sister and hushed the harried one. How many times have we let ourselves be consumed by the tyranny of the moment when we should have been sitting quietly at the feet of Jesus, basking in his peace?

Galatians 5:22-23

Peace. What a rare commodity in our society! Do you know anyone who truly exudes an air of serenity and peace? Isn't it wonderful to be in such a person's presence? To be calmed by the person's utter trust that God reigns over his universe? Lady Julian of Norwich, an exceptional Christian, penned this in the fourteenth century: "All shall be well, and all shall be well, and all manner of things shall be well." That's peace that only the Holy Spirit can give. It's high on Paul's list. It's there for you. Are you resting in it?

UNDERSTANDING YOUR KIDS

Kids won't have the tiniest bit of trouble relating to Luke 10:38-42. They're intimately familiar with siblings' uncanny ability to annoy each other. A work mate recently confessed that when she and her twin were growing up, as they went to sleep they would let their arms hang into the area between their beds just to violate each other's space. My husband and I always have marveled at how sibling snippiness is magnified in the space crunch of camping in a small tent or pop-up trailer. I'll never forget my son's complaint about my daughter: "Mom, Christy's *breathing.*" We gently reminded him that though the slight wheeze might not be pleasing to him, the intake and expulsion of air are necessary for the sustenance of life. We also suggested that he focus on the much louder cricket that was happily ensconced in his corner of the tent. (I wonder if Martha ever complained, "Mom, Mary's *breathing.*")

We need to challenge children to learn to be at peace with others as well as within themselves. Picture the intense sensory overload of a video arcade, a house in which the TV never goes off, a blasting boombox. Kids love it! Many kids can't be comfortable without some kind of noise. But all this distraction is the product of the last few decades. Kids need to learn what it's like to unplug, decompress, and, as they would put it, "chill." They have a wonderful opportunity during those rare quiet moments to hear the voice of God to which Mary was so attuned.

ATTENTION GRABBER The Lesson

All Worked Up

Have kids sit around a table or in a circle.

Say: **Today I'm going to give you a chance to see one another as you've never seen one another before. In fact, you may never see one another this way again! I'm going to show you how to get all worked up. We'll take it step by step, but first you have to learn two very important signals.**

When I hold up my hands and shake them like this (hold your arms straight over your head and shake your hands as rapidly as you can), **that's your signal to get all worked up. But when I clap three times and rest my hands like this** (clap three times; then rest your hands across your chest), **that's your signal to chill out. To chill out, just let your whole body turn to rubber and droop. Let's try that. Pause as kids relax. That's right— just let yourself turn to rubber. Very good.**

Now to get all worked up, the first thing you'll need is bubble gum. Everyone gets two pieces. Toss handfuls of gum until each child has two pieces. **Great. When I give the signal to get all worked up, start blowing as many bubbles as you can. Then shake your hands as I did and wave your arms back and forth at the same time.** Pause for kids to try that; then give the chill-out signal. **Good. Now do the arms and bubbles and blink as fast as you can.** Pause as kids try this. **Very good! Now there's just one more thing to add, and that's tiny little running steps with your feet. Stay in your chair and just pick up your feet and put them down as fast as you can.** Pause as kids try that. Then ask:

● **Do you think you can do all those things at once?** (Yeah!; no, I think I'll get confused.)

Say: **One of the people in our Bible story today got seriously worked up, so I hope you'll put your best effort into this. I also hope you'll put your best effort into chilling out, because the other character in our story was calm and serene.**

OK—here's a test run.

Raise your arms, shake your hands, and ask:

● **What will you do when I do this?** (Get all worked up.)

Clap three times; then rest your hands across your chest and ask:

● **And what will you do when I do this?** (Chill out.)

Say: **Excellent. Now move your chairs into two rows facing each other so you can have the benefit of seeing how wonderful the others look**

TEACHER TIP

For a little extra fun, ask if kids think you can do all the actions at once. Make them promise to give you a standing ovation if you can pull it off. Then get all worked up and give them a chance to see you as they've never seen you before!

when they're all worked up. Now be on your toes, because I'm going to give separate signals to each group.

Alternate giving the get-all-worked-up and chill-out signals. Have the two groups doing the opposite thing most of the time. Include one full minute when both groups are all worked up so kids really have a chance to get worn out and frazzled. Finish by having both groups chill out for a few seconds. Then turn on a CD of ocean surf or serene worship music, and give kids the following commands in a soothing voice:

● **Take a long, slow, deep breath...now slowly exhale.** Repeat.

● **Let your head fall forward; then slowly and gently roll it toward your left shoulder...then your right shoulder.**

● **Take another deep breath...and slowly exhale.**

● **When your body feels heavy and fully relaxed, sit up and look at me.** Ask:

● **Which did you prefer—being all worked up or chilling out? Explain.** Let several children state their preferences.

Then say: **You know, God made each of us different. Some of us like to go, go, go and not slow down for a minute. Others have a less high-energy personality and enjoy doing things that are calm and quiet. Most people probably like a little of both—quiet times and rowdy times. Turn to a partner and tell which kind of person you are—active, quiet, or a little of both.** Pause as kids share, then ask:

● **How many go, go, go, high-energy people do we have?**

● **How many quiet people?**

● **How many who are a little of both?**

Tell kids what your personal style tends to be. Then ask:

● **Did you ever experience a time you were all worked up, even though you didn't want to be, and you just couldn't seem to calm down? What was that like?** Let several students share their experiences.

Say: **Today we're going to learn that God wants us to be at peace. Our Bible story is about a woman who was trapped in hyper mode. And because her sister was the quiet type, the hyper sister became really frustrated—so frustrated, in fact, that she tried to get Jesus on her side. Can you imagine having Jesus settle a squabble between you and your brother or sister? Let's find out what happened.**

BIBLE STUDY

A Tale of Two Sisters (Luke 10:38-42)

Before class, make two photocopies of the "Tale of Two Sisters" story (pp. 71-72), and give them to two girls in the class who are expressive readers.

TEACHER TIP

If you prefer, you may read the sisters' parts yourself. You might want to bring two scarves to drape around your head—one as a costume for Martha and the other as a costume for Mary. Simply change scarves and modify your voice a bit as you switch from sister to sister.

A Tale of Two Sisters

Martha: We're a fortunate family—I can tell you that. When Jesus comes to our little village, do you know where he stays? At *our* house! I live here in Bethany with my brother, Lazarus, and my sister, Mary. When Jesus comes to town, there's so much to be done. You realize, of course, that he brings his best friends with him. There are Peter, James, John, Matthew, and—well, you know—the rest of the Twelve. Do you have any idea how much those men eat? Of course, I am known as the best hostess in Bethany. I brush my grilled fish with just a bit of olive oil and sprinkle on just the right herbs. Mmm-mmm. None of that fishy taste, you know. And my roasted lamb? It just melts in your mouth. And my fig cakes? Well, just let it be said that there isn't a single neighbor who hasn't asked for the recipe.

Mary: We're so honored that Jesus comes to stay with us. Think of it—the Messiah we've waited for all these years chooses our house to rest in. When he's here, he fills the house with love. Every word that he speaks seems to go straight to my soul. I understand things that I never thought I could—and yet there are so many things I don't understand. I want to stay close and catch everything Jesus says. Missing a single word would be like dropping a jewel and letting it roll into the mud. I wish I could explain what a privilege it is to sit and listen to the Son of God. I wish I could share the experience with you.

Martha: You know, the longer we know Jesus, the more people he seems to bring with him. It's only natural—everyone wants to see him, touch him, be healed. But can you imagine what it's like to try to run a household in the midst of all that? Fortunately, our friends and neighbors help. They bring in food, invite some of the disciples to stay at their homes—that kind of thing. I don't know what I'd do without them, because I certainly don't get much help from my sister, Mary. Why, when Jesus gets here, she just kind of goes into a daze. She sits dreamily at his feet, not noticing how much there is to do.

Mary: Jesus is here again! I'm so glad! I've had the strangest feeling lately that he's not going to be with us much longer. There's a sadness about him today, as if he's struggling with what's ahead. I don't understand why he would struggle—after all, he's the Son of God. He can do anything. But he knows that something is about to happen, something that will be difficult for him—I'm sure of it. I can just see the sadness in his eyes. I'm glad he's come to us. He can find some peace and quiet here among his closest friends. I'll stay right here close beside him. Who knows when we'll get to see him again?

(continued on page 72)

Martha: Well! This is just the outside of enough! I have all these people to feed, including the Lord himself, and what does Mary do? She sits there. Sits! Can you believe it? I've worn myself to a frazzle. I've had to organize the food that's coming in from the neighbors. There are extra sleeping mats to be gathered and our best dishes to be put out for the meal. I started cleaning this morning as soon as it was light and barely had the house ready when Jesus arrived. Someone has to get fruit at the market, and I still have bread to bake. Do you think little Miss Mary might at least start the fire? No! She sits by Jesus as if she's the queen of the scene. I've had it. I'm going to say something.

Have everyone give the two girls (or you) a round of applause. Then say: **Martha is about to complain to Jesus about her sister. Can you believe it? Let's find her exact words in Luke 10:40.**

Have a volunteer look up and read Martha's complaint. Ask:

● **How do you think Jesus will respond?** Let kids offer their opinions.

● **Do you sometimes go to your parents if you're angry with your brother or sister? What do they usually do?** (Try to decide what's fair; tell us to work it out.)

● **Do you think you'd have gone to Jesus with a complaint like that? Why or why not?** (No, I'd be embarrassed; I'd try to work it out myself; I wouldn't want Jesus to think I was crabby and couldn't get along with people.)

Say: **Well, let's see what Jesus did about it. We can find his response in Luke 10:41-42. Who would like to read that?**

After a volunteer reads the passage aloud, ask:

● **Why do you think Jesus responded the way he did?** (Because he was disappointed in Martha; because he knew Mary was doing something more important.)

● **How do you think his words made Martha feel?** (She was probably really embarrassed; she might have cried.)

● **What was Martha doing wrong?** (She was too hyper about taking care of meals and things; she cared more about getting things ready than she did about what Jesus was saying.)

● **What was Mary doing right?** (She was spending time with Jesus; she was paying attention to what Jesus was saying.)

Say: **The problem was that Martha let herself get all worked up. All she could think about was everything that had to be done. That seemed more important than spending time with Jesus. Martha lost her sense of peace because of her busyness. She didn't take time to put Jesus first. Mary, on the other hand, treasured every second with her Lord. She sat peacefully at Jesus' feet, and that pleased Jesus more than all of Martha's work. God wants us to be at peace and to put him first whether we're sitting quietly like Mary or serving actively like Martha.**

LIFE APPLICATION

Time Out With Jesus

Before class, photocopy the "Pocketful of Peace" handout (p. 76). Use an X-Acto knife to open the slit at the top of the handouts. Ask:

● **What can we learn from "A Tale of Two Sisters"?** (That it's good to spend time with Jesus; that it's bad to be too busy for Jesus.)

● **Does this story teach us that it's bad to be busy serving others?** (No, it's just bad to let yourself get out of control; no, it's good to serve others, but with the right attitude.)

● **How do you think we can be more like Mary and less like Martha?** (By spending more time reading Jesus' words; by not letting ourselves get too busy.)

● **When do you tend to get too busy and hyper?** (When I've got soccer practice and a lot of homework; when I watch too much TV, then don't have time for everything else.)

Say: **Our lives are much busier and noisier than our great-grandparents' lives were. Because of fast food and electronic appliances, we can cram much more into our days than people could sixty or seventy years ago. But God designed us with a need for quiet time with him.**

● **How would your life be different if you were totally unplugged, if you had no electronic devices whatsoever?** (Things would be a lot quieter; I'd probably be bored; I'd have more time because of not watching TV.)

● **We can't sit at Jesus' feet as Mary did, but how can we spend time with God?** (By going to church; by reading our Bibles; by praying.)

● **At the times you've felt God's presence, what kinds of things were you usually doing?**

Say: **The third fruit of the Spirit Paul mentions is peace. Mary was at peace; Martha was not.** Ask:

● **If Mary could come here today to tell us how to be at peace, what do you think she might say?** (Don't let things that aren't important take over your life; spend quiet time with God.)

Say: **Our craft this week is a cool little tool that can help us learn to be at peace the way Mary was.**

Distribute the "Pocketful of Peace" handout (p. 76). Have kids cut out the pocket on the heavy lines, then fold it so the printing is on the inside. Demonstrate how to fold the right side to the center, the left side to the center, and the bottom flap up. Then fold the top flap down, and tuck the point into the slit in the top flap. Have kids write their names on their handout, and decorate the outside so it looks like a pocket.

COMMITMENT

Peace to You

Say: **Let's go through this handout step by step and learn how to use it. First, scatter around the room so no one is sitting near you.** As students do this, begin to play a CD of ocean surf or soft, peaceful worship music. Then say: **Now open the top and bottom flaps of your handout. Who would like to read what's written at the bottom?** After a volunteer has read the bottom flap aloud, say: **Open the left flap. This section tells us how to find peace with God.** Have a volunteer read that section aloud. **We'll stop for just a few seconds for you to think about these words and pray.**

After a few seconds, have a volunteer read the middle section aloud. Pause again for reflection and prayer. Finally, have another volunteer read the last section aloud. Say: **If you were using this at home, you would turn to your Bible and read Jesus' words at this point. But today, I'll read to you. Please place your handout on the floor behind you, and listen to these words from Scripture. Close your eyes as you listen to me read. The first** few verses are from the Old Testament.

"Be still before the Lord and wait patiently for him" (Psalm 37:7).

"Those who love your laws have great peace of heart and mind and do not stumble" (Psalm 119:165, TLB).

"He will keep in perfect peace all those who trust in him, whose thoughts turn often to the Lord!" (Isaiah 26:3).

Then say: Now hear these words of Jesus.

"Peace I leave with you; my peace I give you. I do not give to you as the world gives. Do not let your hearts be troubled and do not be afraid" (John 14:27).

"I have told you these things, so that in me you may have peace. In this world you will have trouble. But take heart! I have overcome the world" (John 16:33).

And finally, hear the words of Paul, the apostle who taught us that the third fruit of the Spirit is peace.

"Let the peace of Christ rule in your hearts, since as members of one body you were called to peace. And be thankful" (Colossians 3:15).

"And the peace of God, which transcends all understanding, will guard your hearts and your minds in Christ Jesus" (Philippians 4:7).

"Now may the Lord of peace himself give you peace at all times and in every way. The Lord be with all of you" (2 Thessalonians 3:16).

CLOSING

A Peaceful Parting

Stop the CD, gather kids in a group, and ask:

● **Why does God want us to be at peace?** (Because that's when God can speak to us; because it's good for us.)

Say: **Turn to a neighbor and tell how you will spend peaceful moments with Jesus this week.** Encourage kids to plan a quiet time when they get up in the morning, just before bed at night, or at another convenient time.

Say: **Today we're going to finish our lesson in a peaceful way.** Ask:

● **What three fruits of the Spirit have we learned about so far?** (Love, joy, and peace.)

Say: **Let's ask God to bless our lives with those things as we close.** Pray: **Dear Lord, thank you for Mary's example. Please give us your peace, and help us find time to spend peaceful moments with you. We ask for your love and joy in our lives as well. Please help us open our hearts to you so your Holy Spirit can work in us. In Jesus' name, amen.**

Remind kids to take their "Pocketful of Peace" handouts with them.

A Pocketful of Peace

3. Peaceful Moments With Jesus

Find a Bible with Jesus' words printed in red. Turn to the Gospels, the books of Matthew, Mark, Luke, and John. Choose anyplace in those books to begin reading, and read Jesus' words by "reading the red." Read aloud; then pause to think about what you've read, as if Jesus were talking to you.

Pray and ask God to help you to understand Jesus' words and to live by them.

2. Peace With Yourself

Read aloud these words of Jesus:

"Come to me, all you who are weary and burdened, and I will give you rest. Take my yoke upon you and learn from me, for I am gentle and humble in heart, and you will find rest for your souls. For my yoke is easy and my burden is light" (Matthew 11:28-30).

Are there things that are worrying you?

Pretend to hold those things in your hands.

Pray and ask Jesus to take the worries from you.

Jesus knew how important it was for his followers to get away and spend time with him. After a busy day he told them, "Come with me by yourselves to a quiet place and get some rest" (Mark 6:31).

This is your invitation to a quiet time with Jesus.

1. Peace With God

Quietly think back over the last few days. Have you done something you're sorry for? Ask Jesus to forgive that sin right now.

"Create in me a new, clean heart, O God, filled with clean thoughts and right desires. Restore to me again the joy of your salvation, and make me willing to obey you" (Psalm 51:10, 12 TLB).

Believe that you are forgiven and at peace with God.

The Wall That Couldn't Be Stopped

8

LESSON AIM

To help kids understand that ★ we can trust God to help us.

OBJECTIVES

Kids will
- solve a difficult challenge and be rewarded with a treat,
- learn how Nehemiah faithfully relied on God to complete the overwhelming task of rebuilding the wall of Jerusalem,
- identify times they need patience and faithfulness,
- make a pop-up craft depicting the wall of Jerusalem, and
- commit to trusting God to help them be patient and faithful.

YOU'LL NEED

- ❑ an enticing treat
- ❑ an adult or teenage helper to be a clownish doubter
- ❑ clown makeup (optional)
- ❑ clownish clothing (optional)
- ❑ masking tape
- ❑ several sheets of paper
- ❑ photocopies of the "Jerusalem Wall" handout (p. 86)
- ❑ photocopies of the "Jerusalem Pop-Up" (p. 87)
- ❑ scissors
- ❑ glue sticks
- ❑ five paper plates labeled one through five

BIBLE BASIS

Nehemiah 1:1–6:16

King Nebuchadnezzar of Babylon conquered the city of Jerusalem in 597 B.C., transported ten thousand leaders and craftsmen to Babylon, and left a puppet government in place. When the puppet king Zedekiah became rebellious in 588 B.C., Nebuchadnezzar marched against the city again, and this time he ordered complete and systematic destruction that left the crown jewel of Judaism a smoldering wreck. Soldiers torched and looted the city, demolished the Temple, and reduced the great limestone wall to a pile of cracked and blackened rubble. So it lay for well over a century.

Gradually certain Jewish exiles rose to prominence under the Assyrian and Persian kings who bound them to servitude. Nehemiah was such a man. As cupbearer to King Artaxerxes, Nehemiah saw to it that the wine that came to the king's table was safe and free of poison—a responsible post in an empire fraught with intrigue. But while Nehemiah served the Persian king faithfully, his heart longed for the city of David, the home of his faith, his ancestors, and his long-oppressed countrymen. After much prayer, Nehemiah approached the king with a proposal to return to Jerusalem and erase the city's shame by rebuilding its walls. God blessed Nehemiah, and the king granted Nehemiah's request for safe passage back to Judah and for all the materials needed for the job. Way to go, cupbearer!

But Nehemiah's formidable task had just begun. If you've not read the book of Nehemiah in the last twelve months, read it now! Nehemiah's leadership is sheer inspiration from page to page. He sought God's help and blessing at every step. He was patient. He knew when to act and when to wait. He waited for God's perfect timing to present his wild idea to the king. He was faithful. He assigned tasks wisely, defended the city as the walls went up, took care of the poor, tirelessly oversaw the entire operation, and accomplished the rejoining of the wall in fifty-two days! Wow. You'll be blessed by Nehemiah's story, and so will your kids.

Galatians 5:22-23

Imagine the thrill of working with someone who patiently had waited on God's timing until it was a good day to show a sad face to a king. Then imagine the adrenalin rush of taking on the gargantuan task of rebuilding the wall, faithfully bringing this plan to fruition in the face of powerful and determined enemies. Nehemiah waited...then he worked! And that's what God calls us to do as well. Pray patiently. Don't twitch a muscle until God says, "Go!" Then get into gear and kick up some dust! You've got to love Nehemiah. While he majored in patience and faithfulness, you'll find all the other fruit of the Spirit evidenced in his life as well. I'd work for him—wouldn't you?

UNDERSTANDING YOUR KIDS

Once, watching a third-grade boy who simply could not contain himself, I realized that there was an alarm going off in his head, saying "Now! Now! Now!"

It filled me with sadness to realize that this child could make himself so obnoxious that most adults would cave in and give him what he wanted just for the sake of gaining a few moments of peace. Children with attention deficits and very young children tend to live in the "eternal now." The present moment fully occupies them—past and future have little significance. Concepts such as patience and faithfulness come slowly, but come they must! A great deal of the process of growing up involves learning to delay gratification.

For kids in your class, patience and faithfulness translate to not touching the television remote control until homework's done, saving allowance and birthday money for a much-desired Lego set, and finishing household jobs before they invite friends over. There are few lessons in maturity more important than learning to wait for God's timing and working hard over a long period to accomplish an important goal. Nehemiah's story can help kids understand that when they remain faithful, God can and will help them accomplish great things.

ATTENTION GRABBER   The Lesson

Paper Trail

Arrange for an adult or teenage helper to visit your class as a comic character. It's fun (but not absolutely necessary) to have the helper wear clown makeup and one or two outrageous articles of clothing. Tell the helper to stay out of sight until you give the signal for him or her to appear. At that point the helper will pop out and, in gentle good humor, make doubting comments about the kids' ability to accomplish the challenge you've given them.

Bring to class an enticing treat such as warm, fragrant cinnamon rolls, a plate of fresh strawberries, or another treat that you know is a favorite of your students. Show off the treat as students arrive, but explain that no one can enjoy the treat until kids have worked together to accomplish a task. Then place the treat at one end of your classroom, and have all the students gather at the other end. Lay a masking tape line on the floor where students are gathered, and make it clear that no one can cross that line without permission.

Say: **Here's your challenge. I have a wonderful treat for you and I'm very eager to share it. But you're going to have to get to it. You're *all* going to have to get from here to the treat before anyone can enjoy it. Here's the first catch: No one's feet can touch the floor.** Hold up two sheets of paper. **The only things your feet can touch are these two sheets of paper. And here's the second catch: No one can carry anyone else.**

Place the two sheets of paper on the floor just past the masking tape line. Then say: **That's it. Those are all the instructions I have for you.** Sit down and see how kids react to the challenge. If they seem totally stumped, encourage them to brainstorm solutions to their problem. You may need to drop hints

TEACHER TIP

If you have a small room, move to a fairly long hallway for this activity. Set up the activity so that kids must travel at least fifteen feet to reach the treat.

such as "Suppose you stepped on one sheet, then picked it up and moved it..." and "I wonder how many people's feet could fit on one sheet of paper."

At this point, signal your helper to appear. The helper should walk around and shake his or her head and mumble comments such as "They'll never be able to do that" and "Yeah, right. Are they supposed to sprout wings and fly? Flap-flap-flap." The doubting, discouraging comments should be delivered quietly and with humor, and the helper should keep some distance from the children so they won't be intimidated or overly distracted.

While the helper is mumbling, remain quietly supportive. Don't offer information right away. If necessary, guide students to discover that two people can step on one sheet of paper, that they can place the other sheet of paper a foot or two in front of them and step on that one, pick up the paper that's now behind them and move it forward, and so on until they've made their way to the treat. Their combined efforts will be comical and fun to watch! One person will need to go back to the group in the same manner and bring another person to the treat. By continuing with two people going and one person coming back, all the kids will eventually make it to the treat.

Once students have discovered the key to the challenge, the helper should mumble comments such as "Oh, now don't they look silly," "I hope nobody expects *me* to do that," and "Hmph—I guess they think they're pretty smart. *I* would've figured that out a long time ago."

When all the kids finally reach the treat, have the helper say, "Yuck! I never did like that kind of treat. I bet it tastes awful!" Then have him or her make a funny face and storm out of the room.

Congratulate kids as you serve them the treat. Say: **Wow—you guys really hung in there!** Ask:

● **Did you ever doubt that you'd be able to meet my challenge?** (Yes, I thought you'd have to help us; no, I thought we could figure it out.)

● **How did** [name of helper] **affect your determination to reach the treat?** (He made me want to give up; because she mocked us I wanted to try harder.)

Say: **You didn't know it, but in getting to the treat you demonstrated the two fruits of the Spirit we're learning about today: patience and faithfulness.** Ask:

● **How did you show patience?** (By working on a solution until we got one.)

● **How did you show faithfulness?** (By hanging in there; by believing that we could do it.)

Say: **Our Bible story today is about a wall-builder who believed that we can trust God to help us. His name was Nehemiah. And the wall he built required an enormous amount of patience and faithfulness. It wasn't the wall of a house or even a castle or temple. It was a wall around the entire city of Jerusalem. And he wasn't starting from scratch; he was starting with a mess that had been there for nearly 140 years. Let's see what happened.**

Up With the Wall! (Nehemiah 1:1–6:16)

Before class, photocopy the "Jerusalem Wall" pattern (p. 86). Place a sheet of blank paper underneath the copied pattern. The pattern and the sheet behind it eventually will be cut to create four wall sections. Ask:

● **Can anyone tell me the names of the first three kings of God's people?** (I have no clue; Saul, David, and Solomon.)

Say: **When God's people begged for a king, God gave them Saul. But Saul disobeyed God, so God made David king in his place. David was a great king.** Ask:

● **What can you tell me about David?** (He started out as a shepherd; he played the harp for Saul; he killed Goliath; he wrote part of the book of Psalms.)

Say: **David also built up the city of Jerusalem, which he used as his capital. To this day, Jerusalem is called the city of David. After David, came his son Solomon, who continued to build Jerusalem. Solomon's most famous building project was God's Temple. After David and Solomon, came a series of kings—some good and some bad. The bad kings led God's people away from God and taught them to worship idols. Through the prophets, God warned his people they would be punished. They would be invaded and conquered by foreign kings, and their beautiful city would be destroyed.**

And that's exactly what happened. Five hundred eighty-six years before Jesus was born, King Nebuchadnezzar of Babylon invaded Jerusalem and destroyed God's Temple. He burned the city and had his soldiers tear down the walls. So the city of David was left to lie in ruins for well over a hundred years.

All the leaders of God's people were marched hundreds of miles to Babylon, where they served the Babylonian and Persian kings. While they were in captivity, they kept the memories of their homeland alive through songs and stories. Some of the Jews rose to be important people in their new land. Nehemiah was such a man.

Nehemiah held the important position of cupbearer to King Artaxerxes. Ask:

● **Does anyone have a clue about what a cupbearer might do?** Let kids guess.

Say: **It was actually an important position of great trust. The cupbearer tasted the wine that came to the king's table to make sure it wasn't poisoned. Many kings of the Persian empire lost their lives through plots and intrigues at court, so the cupbearer needed to be a man of extreme loyalty who couldn't be bribed at any price.**

Nehemiah served the king faithfully, but his heart was elsewhere. He thought of Jerusalem lying in ruins, and the thought made him sad. He longed to go to the homeland he'd never seen. King Artaxerxes noticed his sad face and asked, "Why do you look so sad?"

Nehemiah had been praying for a long time about his desire to return to Jerusalem. He realized that God might be ready to answer his prayers, so he replied, "May the king live forever!" (That's how you spoke to a king in those days if you didn't want your head chopped off!) "How can I not be sad when the city where my ancestors are buried lies in ruins?"

"What do you want?" the king asked.

Nehemiah sent up a quick prayer, then asked the king to let him go back to Jerusalem and rebuild the city walls. The king gave his permission! And besides that, he gave letters to the governors along the way with instructions to protect Nehemiah while he traveled and to give him the wood he would need for constructing the gates.

Nehemiah was overjoyed! He'd prayed for this opportunity for a long time, and finally God made it happen.

After a long trip, Nehemiah arrived in Jerusalem. He rode around the city and looked at all the places that needed repair. You can't imagine what a mess he found. Huge boulders had tumbled in every direction. They were charred and cracked from the fires so long ago. All the rubble and useless rock would have to be cleared away before the new walls could even begin to go up. But when Nehemiah told the people who lived there about his plan to repair the wall, they were excited and glad to help with the work.

Fold the pattern and the sheet of paper behind it in half along the dotted line.

Nehemiah organized different groups of families to work on different sections of the wall.

Cut from A to B.

But Sanballat and Tobiah, two enemies of God's people, made trouble for the people building the wall.

Cut from C to D, then from D to E and from D to F.

Despite the threats of their enemies, the people faithfully kept on building. They worked with all their hearts because they knew this was God's work.

Cut slits 1 and 2; then open the gates.

And little by little the wall grew.

Separate the four wall sections, and fasten two of them together.

Then Sanballat and Tobiah decided to get an army together and attack Jerusalem. So Nehemiah posted guards all around the wall. Half the people worked while the other half kept watch, ready to fight. Nehemiah said to everyone, "Don't be afraid of our enemies. Remember, God is with us."

So the people kept working faithfully, and the wall grew some more.

Add the third section of the wall.

Everyone worked from the first light of morning until the stars came out at night.

Add the last section of the wall, and fasten it to the first section, creating a circle.

At last the wall was finished! Nehemiah and his helpers were so faithful in their work that rebuilding the wall around the entire city took just fifty-two days! Here's what Nehemiah wrote when the wall was completed:

"So the wall was completed on the twenty-fifth of Elul, in fifty-two days. When all our enemies heard about this, all the surrounding nations

82

were afraid and lost their self-confidence, because they realized that this work had been done with the help of our God" (Nehemiah 6:15-16).

Let's have a big round of applause for Nehemiah and his helpers!

Lead kids in a round of applause; then ask:

● **How did Nehemiah demonstrate patience?** (He waited for just the right moment to ask for the king's permission.)

● **What does it mean to be faithful?** (To hang in there because you know God wants you to; to keep plugging away at a hard job.)

● **How did Nehemiah demonstrate faithfulness?** (He didn't give up when the job looked too hard; he kept working and kept counting on God to help him.)

● **What kinds of discouragement did Nehemiah face?** (The task was so big; enemies tried to stop him.)

● **How were Sanballat and Tobiah like the person who made fun of you earlier in our lesson?** (They tried to stop him; they made fun of him and threatened him.)

● **Why weren't they successful in stopping him?** (He kept trusting God to help him; he believed God was on his side.)

● **How did God help Nehemiah? Let's name all the ways we can think of.** Help kids come up with a list similar to this one: God answered Nehemiah's prayer to go to Jerusalem and caused the king to cooperate with him; God helped him understand how to organize the job; God helped the people work from dawn 'til dark; God protected them from their discouraging enemies; God helped them finish the wall in an amazingly short time.

Say: **Nehemiah believed that when we're patient and faithful, we can trust God to help us.**

LIFE APPLICATION

How Tough Is It?

Say: **Now I'd like you to close your eyes and think really hard.** Ask:

● **When was the last time someone said to you, "Be patient"?** Allow kids to respond.

Say: **Let's have some fun discovering when you struggle with patience and faithfulness.**

Place five paper plates labeled one through five across the floor of your room, with one being at the far left side and five being at the far right.

Say: **I'm going to read a list of things you might have to do. If you would have a lot of trouble being patient and faithful doing that task, stand somewhere between numbers three and five. If you wouldn't have a problem with that task at all, stand closer to number one. Got that? Five means you'd have lots of trouble being patient and faithful; one means you wouldn't have a problem at all. You can stand anywhere between those numbers.**

Read the following list, pausing between each item for kids to rate how much they would struggle with being patient and faithful at that task. To encourage kids to be honest, participate in the activity by placing yourself along the continuum as well.

How difficult is it for you to be patient and faithful when you're
- **doing your math homework?**
- **cleaning your room?**
- **practicing a musical instrument?**
- **writing a big report?**
- **memorizing spelling words?**
- **helping a younger child?**
- **saving your money to buy something you really want?**
- **waiting your turn to play a video game?**
- **dusting or vacuuming your house?**
- **trying to be nice to someone who isn't very nice to you?**
- **helping out at home when all the rest of your friends are playing?**
Ask:

● **Is it important to be patient and faithful in all those things? Why or why not?** (Yes, because then people will trust you with bigger things; yes, because you're obeying God and teachers and parents; no, because they're not really important.)

Say: **Listen to these words of Jesus from Luke 16:10: "Whoever can be trusted with very little can also be trusted with much, and whoever is dishonest with very little will also be dishonest with much."** Ask:

● **Why is it important to God that we're patient and faithful in everything that he gives us to do?** (Because then he can trust us with more; because we're setting a good example of what Christians are like.)

Say: **The good news is that we're not on our own. When we're patient and faithful, we can trust God to help us, just as he helped Nehemiah. Let's make a craft that will remind us of that.**

COMMITMENT

Faithfully Yours
Make a sample "Jerusalem Pop-Up" card before class.

Distribute photocopies of the "Jerusalem Pop-Up" pattern (p. 87). Show the kids your completed sample, and say: **We're going to make a 3-D model of the Jerusalem wall.**

Show kids how to fold the pattern in half on Line 1. Have them cut from the middle dot to the outside dot on the middle and bottom lines of the city. The top line of the city should remain uncut—it becomes the background when the card is finished. When the two cuts are made, have kids fold down on Line 2. Show them how to rub a little glue around the background at the top and bottom of the city, then press the outline of the city into place against the back of the card.

Demonstrate how to pull the city gently forward and pull the card back so the center of the card becomes a valley fold and the city pops forward. To give the city more dimension, fold forward (valley folds) at the two edges, fold back (mountain folds) at the first tower, fold forward (valley folds) at the inner edge of the first tower, and fold back (mountain folds) at both edges of the center tower.

When the folds are done correctly, the city will fold back into the card when it's closed and pop out when the card is opened.

When the cards are finished, have kids read aloud the verse that's printed above the city: "So the wall was completed...in fifty-two days. When all our enemies heard about this, all the surrounding nations were afraid and lost their self-confidence, because they realized that this work had been done with the help of our God" (Nehemiah 6:15-16). Ask:

● **How can this card encourage you to be faithful?** (It can help me remember that Nehemiah was patient and faithful and finished a hard job; it can remind me that God will help me.)

Say: **Turn to a partner and tell one way that you'll be patient and faithful this week.** After kids have shared, tell them one way *you'll* be patient and faithful.

CLOSING

Fruit Rap-Up
Say: **Patience and faithfulness are two qualities in Paul's list called the...** (allow kids to respond) **fruit of the Spirit! You'll find the whole list on the back of your Jerusalem Pop-Up. Let's sing our song and review the fruit of the Spirit together.**

The Fruit of the Spirit
(to the tune of "Rock Around the Clock")

Love and joy.
Love, joy, peace.
In your heart may they increase.
We're talking patience, kindness, goodness, too.
And faithfulness to last your whole life through.
Gentleness and self-control—
The fruit God's Spirit grows in you!
(Repeat)

Close with a prayer similar to this one: **Lord, it's not easy to be patient and faithful, but we know that we can trust you to help us. Thank you for the story of Nehemiah and for the great things he accomplished for you. Help us to be patient and faithful this week in the small things we have to do so that someday we may be able to do great things for your kingdom. In Jesus' name we pray, amen.**

Remind kids to take their Jerusalem Pop-Up cards with them.

JERUSALEM WALL

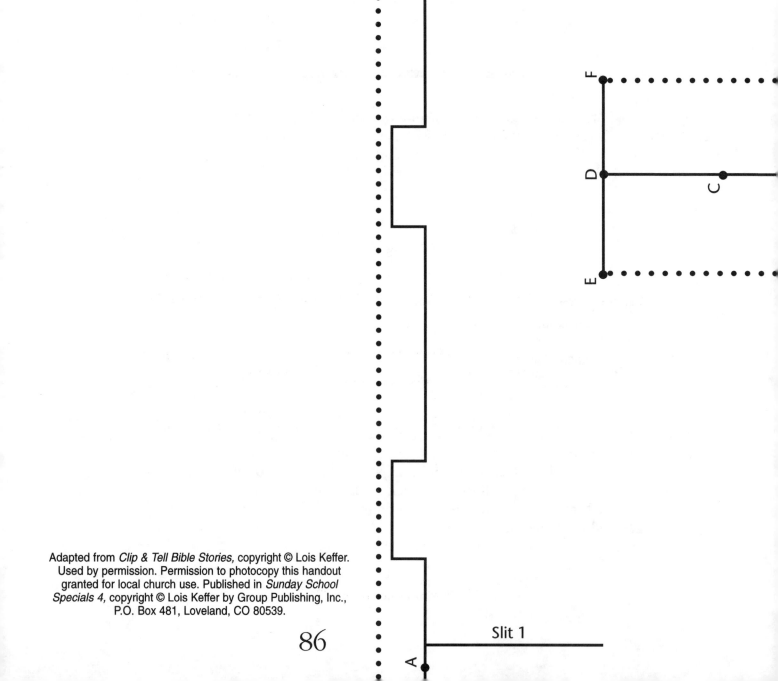

B

Slit 2

F

D

C

E

Slit 1

A

The Fruit of the Spirit
(to the tune of "Rock Around the Clock")

Love and joy.
Love, joy, peace.
In your heart may they increase.
We're talking patience, kindness, goodness, too.
And faithfulness to last your whole life through.
Gentleness and self-control—
The fruit God's Spirit grows in you!
(Repeat)

Line 1

**When we're patient
and faithful, we can
trust God to help us.**

JERUSALEM POP-UP

Line 2

"So the wall was completed…
in fifty-two days.
When all our enemies heard about this,
all the surrounding nations were afraid and lost their self-confidence,
because they realized that this work had been done with the help of our God"

(Nehemiah 6:15-16).

9 Abigail Saves the Day

LESSON AIM

To help kids understand that ★ God's people are gentle and kind.

OBJECTIVES

Kids will:
- go on missions of kindness,
- learn how Abigail's kindness saved the day,
- change harsh responses to kind, gentle responses, and
- create a booklet to help them develop habits of kindness.

YOU'LL NEED

- ❑ party bubbles
- ❑ balloons
- ❑ noisemakers
- ❑ candy bars
- ❑ star stickers
- ❑ self-stick bows
- ❑ an older person to play Abigail's servant
- ❑ a bathrobe, sandals, a tie, and fabric for a Bible-time costume
- ❑ a photocopy of "The Servant's Story" (p. 92-93)
- ❑ red-hot candies, such as Atomic Fire Balls, that will shatter when struck with a hammer
- ❑ large marshmallows
- ❑ a hammer
- ❑ photocopies of the "Be Kinder Reminder" handout (p. 98)
- ❑ scissors

1 Samuel 25:2-42

This story would make great headlines: "Wise Woman Saves Household, Marries Future King." Just consider the characters.

David—gallant, handsome warrior, chosen by God to succeed to the throne of Israel; though hunted, refuses to kill his pursuer even when given the perfect opportunity to do so.

Nabal—the guy you love to hate. Obnoxious, arrogant, filthy rich, foul-mouthed, and stingy as sunshine in March. Married to a lovely woman he doesn't appreciate.

Abigail—intelligent, wise, God-fearing, humble, willing to serve, and drop-dead gorgeous.

And a cast of hundreds—fighting men, shepherds, sheep shearers, and the vast household staff of a wealthy landowner.

David and six hundred of his men had been playing an exhausting game of cat and mouse with Saul. Driven by a jealous desire to guard his throne, Saul hatched plot after plot to capture and kill David. Rather than fighting the Lord's anointed king, David chose to flee and to prove his loyalty by sparing Saul's life. David took refuge in wilderness caves where food for his men was anything but abundant. Rather than plundering the flocks of local landowners—which many warlords would have done—David and his men guarded the interests of the lo-cals. Then, when shearing time came and food and wine were plentiful, David felt justified in asking Nabal to share the bounty.

Nabal was not so inclined. His terse message mocked and belittled David. It's not surprising that David was on a short fuse, exhausted and hungry as he must have been. As he prepared to attack, Nabal's better half made a timely ap-pearance. Not only did Abigail provide for David's men with kindhearted gen-erosity, her gentle spirit and spiritual insight saved David from unnecessary vi-olence. Then God himself dealt with Nabal, leaving David free to take the wise and beautiful Abigail as his wife. In the end, because she saved David's personal integrity, Abigail's wise spiritual counsel became a greater gift than her gener-ous provision of food.

Galatians 5:22-23

We don't often think of kindness, gentleness, and goodness as powerful character traits, but in this instance they certainly won the day. Abigail's wise, sweet-tempered response stilled David's sword and reversed his course of ac-tion—something countless warriors had failed to do. Spirit-directed kindness packs a wallop of love that few can resist. Gentleness disarms anger. Goodness embarrasses pettiness. When the Holy Spirit nurtures these qualities in your life, stand back! You may change the course of history!

It has been said that kindness is the basic language of love. It's certainly a trait that we need to affirm in our kids whenever we see it. Young children tend to be gentle and kind, and most of the time they aspire to be good. By the end of third grade some of that sweetness disappears. And when two more years pass—oh, no!—you have fifth-graders! They sometimes act snotty, often are sarcastic, and can be driven by cliques. What happened?

Partly inspired by developmental changes, and partly by media influences— you won't find a premium on kind, gentle speech and actions in prime time— children yearn to be the master of the put-down. Little cruelties seem funny, and hurt feelings are a small price to pay for stealing the scene. In our homes and churches we need to put everything we have into reversing this trend. Abigail's kindness, gentleness, and goodness made a huge impact in her world. Kids need to understand that, living in the power of the Holy Spirit, they can make a big difference in their worlds. All that is good and kind and gentle can win over all that is mean-spirited. Use this lesson to teach kids that they can be instruments of goodness just as Abigail was.

The Lesson ATTENTION GRABBER

Kindness Raid

Before class, identify two or three people in your church who are favorites with your kids. You might include a teacher, someone who brings treats, a caretaker, a music leader, a favorite "grandpa," or the pastor. Consider warning the individuals you choose that they're in for a pleasant surprise this morning.

As kids arrive, set out the following items to pique their curiosity: one or two bottles of bubbles, star stickers, balloons, self-stick bows, candy bars, and party noisemakers.

Say: **I feel like starting off today with a little adventure. I think it's time our class went on a raid—a kindness raid! Here's the plan: We'll deliver an outpouring of kindness that a couple of lucky people won't soon forget. I've chosen some people I think you'll enjoy surprising—** [name the people].

Here's how our kindness raid will work. First we'll surround the person and clap and cheer. Someone will blow bubbles over his or her head, someone will give a back rub, some will put stickers or a bow on the person, someone will give the person a balloon, someone will give a candy bar, and some will blow noisemakers and offer high fives. Then we'll disappear as quickly as we came and run directly back to our room

and get ready for our next raid. There's one important thing to remember—our object is not to scare the person to death. Our object is to shower our recipients with kindness.

Let kids work together to share the materials and decide who will do what. You may want to let kids switch roles with each raid. If you have a fairly large class, have several kids just clap and cheer. Reassemble in your room after each raid to prepare for the next one. After the last raid, collect all the materials, gather kids in a circle, and ask:

● **What did you think about the way people reacted to our raids?** (They couldn't figure out what was going on; they're not used to that kind of thing.)

● **What was fun about doing a kindness raid?** (It surprised people and made them happy; it was wild and crazy.)

● **In a typical day, do you usually encounter more people who are kind or more people who are rude? Explain.** (It depends on the day; usually most people are crabby.)

● **Do you think Christians tend to be more kind than people who don't know God? What's the reason for that?** (Yes, because they try to be like Jesus; yes, because they want to live as the Bible says to live.)

Say: **Today we're going to learn that God's people are gentle and kind. Our Bible story is about a remarkable woman who went on a kindness raid and headed off a huge disaster. Fortunately, she had a servant who clued her in that something terrible was about to happen...**

BIBLE STUDY

Abigail Saves the Day (1 Samuel 25:2-42)

Before class, recruit an older person in your congregation to visit your class as Abigail's servant. Or "age" a younger person with a gray wig and some wrinkles drawn with makeup. Either a man or woman may play the servant. You'll need a volunteer with lots of personality who can deliver the script with a twist of Jewish humor. Photocopy "The Servant's Story" (pp. 92-93), and give it to the volunteer a few days before class. Encourage him or her to create a Bible-time costume using a bathrobe, sandals, and towels or scarves.

Cue the helper to make a hurried, breathless entrance when you say, "something terrible was about to happen" at the end of the previous activity.

The Servant's Story

Such a mess you've never seen! Do you hear me? There's never been such a mess! Where's the mistress? Get me the mistress, or by this time tomorrow we'll all be history. It's the boss—oy, it's always the boss. He's such a knucklehead! His name is Nabal (NAY-bal). That means fool. Would I kid you? You can read it right in the Bible. Go ahead—look. The fool—that's Nabal. Has he lived up to his name today!

There's David—you know—the one who killed the giant when he was just a little whippersnapper. King Saul has been jealous of him ever since. Everyone knows David will be the next king. Sure—it's a done deal. But Saul, he's not giving up the throne any time soon. He's been chasing David all over the countryside. But can he catch him? Never. The Lord watches over David.

So you think the boss would sit up and take notice. "Be nice to David," he should be thinking. "Soon he'll be our king." But not Nabal. He's so rich he thinks no one can touch him. He has flocks as far as the eye can see. You'd think David and his men would just swoop down and help themselves to a few lamb chops when they get hungry. But no—they watch over the sheep and the shepherds for weeks so no one comes to any harm. Then they ask politely. They wait 'til shearing time when there's food to spare. Now if I were the boss, I'd say, "David, you're like a son to me. All these weeks you've watched over my shepherds and sheep—they've never been so safe. Take all the food you want, and don't go hungry." But not Nabal. He's not so smart. He insults David and sends his servants away.

So what would you do if you were David, sitting up in the hills with six hundred fighting men whose stomachs are growling? I'll tell you. You'd attack and turn Nabal's place into so much mincemeat. Then you'd help yourself to all the food and treasure you could carry. And that's just what's going to happen if I don't find the mistress.

Such a woman, the mistress. Have you seen her? Lovelier than a summer morning, gentle as a lamb. An unkind word never crosses her lips. The smartest woman in three kingdoms, I tell you. She'll fix this. Oy—where's the mistress?

(Leave the room for a moment; then return.)

Oh—it's you again! Still here after almost two weeks? Fine—OK. This is a good place to be.

So where was I? Oh, yes. It's all coming back to me. David and his men were about to attack. But my mistress saved the day. Didn't I tell you she would?

I told her how Nabal had turned away David's servants with no food. I explained how David's men had been like a wall of protection around us night and day, and how Nabal had insulted them.

So kind and good is Abigail! Without saying a word to Nabal, she took two hundred loaves of bread, two skins of wine, five sheep ready for roasting, bags and bags of grain, a hundred cakes of raisins, and two hundred cakes of pressed figs and loaded them on donkeys. She sent me on ahead with the donkeys. Then she followed, and when she saw David, she bowed low to the ground and treated him like a king. She apologized for her foolish husband and asked David for forgiveness. She offered the food as a gift and told David gently that he would be glad not to have the blood of Nabal on his hands.

What could David do but accept her kindness? "Praise be to the Lord, the God of Israel, who has sent you today to meet me," he said. "May you be blessed for your good judgment and for keeping me from bloodshed this day."

Such a woman, mistress Abigail. Her gentle words stopped the angry warrior. All the armies of the Philistines couldn't stop David, but a little kindness from my mistress, and he couldn't turn around fast enough. The next day Abigail told the boss about all the food she'd given to David. And what do you think happened? Old Nabal had a stroke right on the spot, and a few days later he died. God struck him down—that's what happened. Then David sent a messenger asking Abigail to be his wife.

A wedding! A wedding for my mistress! And a kind, gentle wife for David. Oy—I love happy endings!

(Exit.)

Lead kids in a rousing round of applause as the actor exits. Then say: **In Bible times, it was considered common courtesy to offer hospitality to anyone who was in the area—especially among God's people. Bands of fighting men like David's commonly robbed and looted and took whatever they needed. But David's men were honorable. So when Nabal refused to give kindness in return for kindness, David's anger almost got the best of him. Let's find out exactly what Nabal said to David's messengers.**

Have a volunteer look up and read 1 Samuel 25:10-11.

Then say: **Abigail, however, approached David in a much different manner.** Have another volunteer read 1 Samuel 25:23-24, 26-31.

● **Why did Abigail's words calm David's anger?** (She understood him; she apologized and tried to make up for what her husband had said; she honored and respected him.)

● **What reason did Abigail give David for not attacking Nabal?** (She didn't want him to be guilty of revenge; she wanted him to have a clear conscience.)

● **What can we learn from Abigail's words and actions?** (That being kind can fix a bad situation; that you should think of other people's feelings.)

● **Have you ever seen gentle words and kind actions resolve a scary situation? Explain.** Let kids share their experiences.

Say: **God's people are gentle and kind, and Abigail is a perfect role model. Nabal is a perfect example of how *not* to act. His unkindness set the scene for a disaster. But Abigail turned things around. Her words and actions put out the fire of David's anger. Let's see if we can follow her example.**

LIFE APPLICATION

Put Out the Fire

Hold up a red-hot candy, such as an Atomic Fire Ball, and ask:

● **How many of you have had the experience of eating one of these red-hot candies? What is it like?** (Really hot; it burns your mouth like crazy.)

Say: **Let's compare this red-hot candy to hotheaded Nabal.** Hold up a large marshmallow. **And we'll compare this soft, puffy marshmallow to kind, gentle Abigail. Now when something happens to a hotheaded person like Nabal,** (hit the red-hot candy with a hammer—it will shatter into pieces) **stand back! You've got disaster in every direction! Would anyone like a piece of this disaster?** Allow kids who want a piece of the broken candy to take one.

But when something happens to a kind, gentle person like Abigail, (strike the marshmallow with a hammer) **he or she finds a way to bounce back. Proverbs 15:1 tells us, "A gentle answer turns away wrath, but a harsh word stirs up anger."**

● **How was this true in today's Bible story?** (Nabal's nasty response almost got him killed, but Abigail's kind, gentle response saved the day.)

● **How is that true in everyday life?** (If you smart off, you always make things worse; if you try to calm things down, you can usually do it.)

Say: **The Holy Spirit works in God's people to help them be gentle and kind. Let's see how that sounds. I've got some more red-hot candies here. I'm going to toss one to someone and give that person a nasty Nabal statement. Then that person will think of something better to say—something that would calm the situation instead of blowing it out of control. After you've given a better response, I'll toss you a marshmallow. Then other people who want to offer better responses can raise their hands and respond as well.**

Before you read each of the following statements, toss a red-hot candy to a student. When he or she has given a kinder, gentler response, toss him or her a marshmallow. Let other kids offer better responses as well. If you have plenty of marshmallows, toss one to each student who offers a better response.

● **You're such a klutz! I can't believe you broke that!** (Here, let me help you clean that up.)

● **I got a better grade than that, and I didn't even study.** (I'm sorry you're disappointed in your grade.)

● **Where'd you get that outfit—from the dump?** (Do you have a new outfit? It's nice!)

● **Can you believe what a snob she is?** (I've had a hard time getting to know her.)

● **You lose—too bad.** (Good game!)

● **Can't you see I'm busy? Do me a favor and disappear.** (Maybe we could get together another time.)

● **I guess we're stuck with you on our team again.** (Hey—what position would you like to play?)

● **Sorry—our table's full. You'll have to sit somewhere else.** (I think we can squeeze in one more person.)

● **You only got the part because you're the teacher's pet.** (Congratulations on getting the part.)

● **So you had a bad day—pouting won't make it any better.** (I'm sorry you're upset. Can I help?)

● **He's a jerk. I'm glad he got in trouble.** (He may have been asking for it, but I still feel bad for him.)

Share red-hot candies and marshmallows with any students who haven't received them. Then say: **It's one thing to *say* something kind, but it's another thing to *mean* it. That's where goodness comes in. Only God can make us really good inside. And until we allow God to do that, our kind responses may sound fake. But when God has forgiven our sins and filled our hearts with love, the Holy Spirit can work within us to help us be sincerely kind. True kindness is powerful. It can change the whole atmosphere of our families, our neighborhoods, and our schools.**

COMMITMENT

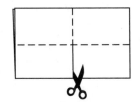

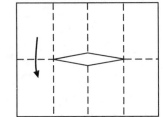

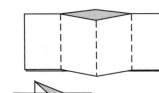

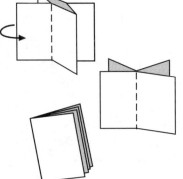

Be Kinder Reminder

Ask:

● **Do you think it's cool to be kind? Explain.** (Yes, I like to be around people who are nice; no, it's wimpy.)

● **Is it cool to be gentle and good? Explain.** (I don't usually think of it that way; yes, because that's what the Bible says to do.)

Say: **Unfortunately, our society puts a lot of value on clever put-downs and smarting off. But those aren't God's values. God's people are gentle and kind. Some people are just naturally kind. But most of us have to work at it a little bit. And practice, as they say, makes perfect.**

Through the years, people have learned that it takes about twenty-one days to develop a new habit—good or bad. I have something for you today that will help you develop a kindness habit. It's called a "Be Kinder Reminder."

Distribute scissors and photocopies of the "Be Kinder Reminder" handout (p. 98) to each student. Demonstrate how to fold and cut the handout to make an eight-page booklet. (See the illustrations in the margin.)

Have kids sign their names on the first page of their booklets.

Say: **Find a partner, and read pages 2 through 4 together. As you read, tell who might appreciate receiving that kind word or action from you.**

Allow a few minutes for partners to read and discuss the booklet.

CLOSING

Tough Stuff

Say: **If you listen to what's said on TV or in the halls at school, you might think it's cool to be cruel. But the truth is, anybody can say something nasty. It's tough to be kind and good. It takes real strength to be gentle. And that strength comes from the Holy Spirit. Let's review our fruit of the Spirit rap and close by asking God's Holy Spirit to help us develop positive habits of kindness, gentleness, and goodness in our lives.**

The Fruit of the Spirit
(to the tune of "Rock Around the Clock")

Love and joy.
Love, joy, peace.
In your heart may they increase.
We're talking patience, kindness, goodness, too.
And faithfulness to last your whole life through.

Gentleness and self-control—
The fruit God's Spirit grows in you!
(Repeat)

Close in prayer. Challenge kids to work with their "Be Kinder Reminder" booklets every day.

KIND THINGS TO SAY

Thank you.

Can I help?

I appreciate that.

That's really nice of you.

I love you.

You're the best!

Good job.

Nice try!

KINDNESS LOG

Starting Date:

I was kind to:

Day 1

Day 2

Day 3

Day 4

Day 5

Day 6

Day 7

Day 8

Day 9

Day 10

Day 11

Day 12

Day 13

Day 14

KINDNESS LOG

Day 15

Day 16

Day 17

Day 18

Day 19

Day 20

Day 21

KIND THINGS TO DO

Share something you treasure.

Be helpful.

Notice people's feelings.

Smile.

Listen.

Write a note.

Express your thanks.

Give a pat on the back.

Encourage someone.

Give a compliment.

BE KINDER REMINDER

This booklet belongs to

Let's Hear It for Job!

LESSON AIM

To help kids understand that ★ God wants us to be thoughtful and wise.

OBJECTIVES

Kids will
- experience how it feels to struggle for control,
- learn how Job remained thoughtful and wise through a series of disasters,
- identify what tempts them to lose control, and
- commit to practicing self-control in everyday life.

YOU'LL NEED

- ❏ masking tape
- ❏ balloons
- ❏ photocopies of the "Control Freak" handout (p. 107)
- ❏ scissors
- ❏ crayons or markers
- ❏ tape

BIBLE BASIS

Job 1-42

Job is a difficult book. (Yes, that's a little like saying ice cream is cold.) It is the first in the five books of Scripture we call the wisdom literature. (The other books are Psalms, Proverbs, Ecclesiastes, and Song of Songs.) Psalms and Proverbs, the greater works of wisdom literature, ring with the peal that God cares for those who love him, that the righteous will flourish and the wicked will struggle and fail. Yet the Psalmist himself turns and laments, "For I envied the arrogant when I saw the prosperity of the wicked" (Psalm 73:3). This is the great conundrum of the wisdom literature: It teaches the great principle that God cares for and upholds the righteous, yet it laments God's seeming lack of care when faithful individuals suffer and those who deny and defy God do well. And that, in a nutshell, is the story of Job. He loves God and God prospers him. Satan accuses God, saying that Job's love is based only on gratitude for all his blessings, and that if those blessings were to be stripped, Job would cease to love God.

So the battle for Job's heart begins. Calamities wipe out Job's family and possessions, ill health attacks his body, and his friends and wife attack his faith and protestations of innocence. Who could possibly withstand the self-righteous babbling of foolish friends without flying into a murderous rage? How could a man watch the systematic disintegration of his life and world without cursing God, abandoning his faith, and becoming a lunatic? Job's dogged self-control is firmly rooted in his tenacious faith in a just and kind creator, God. And through legendary woes, that faith steadies his course until God's blessing is restored.

Galatians 5:22-23

Self-control caps Paul's list of the fruit of the Spirit. Perhaps that's because all the other qualities need to be in place before self-control can finally be achieved. Most people struggle for self-control in some area of their lives, whether it be unwholesome language, eating, spending, watching TV, or the need to overachieve. The Holy Spirit is our ever-present "hound of heaven," always at our elbow, smoothing our jagged edges, polishing our imperfections. As we surrender to the Spirit's guidance, we gradually gain control over those vulnerable areas. What a joy to see progress in our lives, slow though it may be. God grant us the tenacity and patience of his loyal servant, Job.

UNDERSTANDING YOUR KIDS

The media is rife with headlines about kids who are out of control. You've read it all. You've watched the evening news after a school shooting, felt your heart go out to a grieving town, and thought, "How can kids go so wrong so young?"

Long before there was a destructive act, there was a destructive attitude. A hateful mind-set and cruel words precede violence.

Rebellion against God comes in the aftermath of rebellion against parents and teachers. There are compelling reasons to teach kids the virtue of self-control. By the time children grow into nearly adult bodies, they need to be well down the road to learning to control their language, their attitudes, and their appetites.

It's human nature to want to indulge our desires and appetites. It's the Holy Spirit who helps us submit to God's written standards for our lives. Use this lesson to help kids see that while the world says, "Do whatever feels good," God calls us to disciplines that help us lead lives honoring him.

Double-Trouble Challenge

Before class, lay two eight-foot lengths of masking tape on the floor, three inches apart. Set out a bag of uninflated balloons.

As kids arrive, have them form pairs. Pair younger students with older ones, if you have a mixed-age group.

Say: **To start out today, I have a Double-Trouble Challenge for you. Let's see if you're up to it.** Lead children to the masking tape lines. **This challenge is called Fleet Feet. The first thing you'll need to do is decide which partner will be the Spinner and which will be the Runner. When you come to the line and I say "go," if you're the Runner you'll close your eyes and the Spinner will spin you around ten times really fast. The rest of us will count to ten as you spin. Then you'll open your eyes and try to tiptoe down between the two lines as fast as you can without setting a foot outside the lines. I'll be the line judge, and I'll call "out" if a foot goes outside the line. When the first Runner has gone, the next pair will step up to the line and we'll count out loud as the Spinner spins the next Runner.** Ask:

● **Who can explain to me how this challenge works?** Let kids repeat the rules in their own words; then have pairs line up at one end of the masking tape lines. Have kids count out loud enthusiastically as the Spinners spin the Runners. Cheer for the Runners whether or not they step outside the lines. Once all the Runners have finished, have partners switch roles.

Then say: **Great job! Are you ready for the second challenge? It's called the Hot Air Escape. You'll each need to take a balloon, blow it up, and pinch the end.**

Once all the kids are holding their inflated balloons, say: **Now please scatter around the room. When I point to you, hold your balloon over your head and let it go. Your challenge is to prevent it from hitting the floor as it deflates. Ready?**

Point to kids one by one. Keep reminding them not to let their balloons touch the floor. (It's doubtful that any of the kids will be able to accomplish the challenge—deflating balloons are very erratic!) If kids are eager to try again and if you have plenty of time, let kids inflate their balloons once more. This time, have all the kids release their balloons on the count of three. You'll have happy chaos as balloons go zipping in every direction.

Designate a corner where kids can set their balloons aside. They'll need them again later in the lesson. Gather kids in a circle and ask:

● **Did anyone accomplish both our challenges?** It's unlikely that anyone will have succeeded.

Say with a light, teasing expression: **Hmm—I don't understand why these things were so difficult for you.** Hold up a balloon and ask:

● **Aren't you a lot bigger than this little balloon? Why couldn't you**

TEACHER TIP

Have kids who have an easy time blowing up their balloons help those who find it more difficult.

keep your balloon from hitting the floor? (Because it moved too fast; it was faster than I was.)

● **Aren't you smarter than a balloon?** (Yes, but that doesn't help; balloons don't have brains.)

Say: **If you're bigger and smarter than a balloon, I just don't see what the problem is.** Shake your head. **That's very strange. Well, let's go back here where we did the Fleet Feet challenge.** Ask:

● **Do everyone's feet fit inside these lines?** Allow several children to place their feet between the lines.

● **Can anyone walk between these lines right now without stepping outside them?** Let several children demonstrate that they can.

● **Why is it easy now when it was so hard before?** (Because we aren't dizzy; because we didn't spin around.)

● **What difference does being dizzy make?** (It's hard to go straight; it makes you wobbly.)

Say: **Sometimes life is like our Double-Trouble Challenge. Like our zipping balloons, things can happen so quickly that we just can't stay in control. Or, as with our Fleet Feet challenge, our own actions can make us lose control and fail. Our Bible story today is about a man who had everything—absolutely everything!—go wrong. What's amazing is that through all the things that happened, he didn't give up or lose his faith in God. God wants us to be thoughtful and wise. Job is a great example of someone who refused to spin out of control no matter what happened to him.**

BIBLE STUDY

Job the Survivor

Say: **I need your help to tell the Bible story today. Let's begin by forming four groups. We'll count off by fours; then each group will go to a different corner of the room.**

When you have four groups, say: **Group 1, you're the Oxen (which are like cattle) and Donkeys. What do you sound like?** Pause as the kids moo and heehaw. **Group 2, you're the Sheep. What do you sound like?** Pause as they bleat and baa. **Group 3, you're the Camels and, frankly, I don't know what you sound like! Why don't you just try looking humpy?** Encourage kids to pull their arms behind their backs to look like humps. **Group 4, you're the Disasters. I'll tell you how you sound in a minute. Everyone pay close attention to the story, listening for your part, and I'll tell you what to do.**

Once there lived a man named Job. He was the greatest and wealthiest man of his country. He was good, honest, and fair, and he honored God and taught his children to do the same.

One day all of Job's children had gathered for a feast at the home of his oldest son. Then the first disaster hit. A group of Sabean (suh-BEE-un) **raiders** swooped down on all Job's oxen and donkeys and carried them off. Only one servant escaped to tell Job the bad news.

Direct the Disasters to surround the Oxen and Donkeys, circle the room with them, then herd them to the center of the room. Have the Oxen and Donkeys sit down as the Disasters return to their corner.

Shortly after that, the second disaster hit. Lightning fell from the sky and burned up all the sheep. Only one servant escaped to tell Job the bad news.

Direct the Disasters to surround the Sheep, make sounds of thunder, and move their arms like jagged streaks of lightning. Then have them escort the Sheep to the center of the room. Have the Sheep sit down as the Disasters return to their corner.

While that was still happening, three groups of Chaldean (kal-DEE-un) **raiders swooped down on the herds of camels and carried them off. Only one servant escaped to tell Job the bad news.**

Direct the Disasters to surround the Camels, circle the room with them, then herd them to the center of the room. Have the Camels sit down as the Disasters return to their corner.

But this terrible day wasn't over yet. Quickly form two groups from the children who are sitting in the center of the room. **Those of you on this side will represent Job's sons and daughters. The rest of you will stand and form a circle around them to represent the oldest son's house. Raise your arms toward the center of the circle to form a roof.** Pause as the kids you've designated as Job's sons and daughters huddle under the group you've designated to be the house. **Good.**

The last disaster of the day struck. A mighty wind blew up and struck the house where all Job's sons and daughters were feasting. Instruct the Disasters to surround the "house" and blow. **The house collapsed and killed everyone inside.** Instruct the kids who are forming the house to drop to the floor. **Only one servant escaped to tell Job the bad news.**

Have the Disasters join the rest of the kids on the floor. Ask:

● **What do you think Job might have thought after a day like that?** (That he should give up and die; that God had something against him.)

● **What do you think he might have said?** (Something I couldn't repeat; he might have yelled at God.)

Say: **Let's find out from the Bible exactly what Job did say.** Read aloud Job 1:21b: **"The Lord gave and the Lord has taken away; may the name of the Lord be praised." Excuse me? Did Job actually** *praise* **the Lord?** Ask:

● **How could he do that?** (Because he still loved God; I don't know.)

Say: **Let's see if we can make up a situation that would be similar to Job's. It might go something like this: A tornado hits a house and destroys everything, the bank goes broke and suddenly all the money is gone, and a car crash kills all but one person in a family.**

● **If that happened to you, do you think you could praise the Lord at the end of that day?** Allow kids to respond.

● **Have you ever felt really angry at God after something bad happened?** (Yes, when my parents got divorced; no, because I know God loves me.)

Say: **Listen to what else the Bible says about Job that day: "In all this, Job did not sin by charging God with wrongdoing"** (Job 1:22). Ask:

• **Who can put that in your own words?** (Job didn't get mad and say bad things about God; Job didn't blame God for what happened.)

Say: **Well, we're not finished with everything that happened to Job. Before long Job got painful sores all over his body—literally from head to foot. He was so miserable that he sat in an ash pile and scratched his sores with a piece of broken pottery.**

Raise your hand if you've had chickenpox. Do you remember how the sores itch *all* the time? That's how Job felt—only it went on much longer than chickenpox.

Still Job wouldn't say anything against God. His wife, on the other hand, lost it. She came to him and said, "Why don't you curse God and die?" To curse God would be to say terrible things about God. But Job refused to do that. He simply said, "If we're willing to accept good things from God, then we should be able to accept trouble, too."

• **How could Job be so calm after all the things that had happened to him?** (I don't know; because God helped him.)

Say: **God wants us to be thoughtful and wise, and that's exactly what Job was. Despite all the things that happened to him, Job never lost control. Deep in his heart, Job loved and respected God. And even though he was terribly sad, he trusted God and refused to curse God or use God's name in the wrong way.**

And God rewarded Job for his faithfulness. Eventually God blessed Job with a second family and more riches than he had before.

LIFE APPLICATION

In Control

Say: **Job was amazingly thoughtful and wise in the midst of terrible circumstances. But we're not always that way. We all have areas in our lives where it's hard for us to stay in control. Let's explore some of those areas and see how we might conquer them.**

Have kids get their balloons from the Hot Air Escape activity. Be sure to have extra balloons on hand in case kids lose or pop their balloons. Help kids blow up their balloons and pinch the ends.

Say: **Now hang on tight to those balloons. I'm going to read a list. If I name something that's hard for you to control, let a little tiny bit of air out of your balloon. If control in that area is no problem for you, just keep pinching the neck of your balloon, and don't let any air out. The key is to be honest with yourself and not to pay attention to what anyone around you is doing.**

Read the following list, pausing for a moment between each item to let kids respond.

- **watching TV**
- **talking about people behind their backs**
- **eating candy**

TEACHER TIP

If someone accidentally lets all the air out of a balloon, simply have that child reinflate the balloon before you read the next item on the list.

104

- talking back to parents or teachers
- becoming angry at a brother or sister
- playing video games
- putting people down
- using bad language
- making snotty comments
- not always being truthful
- using God's name to swear

Say: **Thank you for being honest with yourself. We all have things we struggle with, and it's not easy to admit it. But when we call ourselves Christians, everything we do and say reflects on Jesus. That's one reason God wants us to be thoughtful and wise. Bad things may happen to us as they did to Job. At first we might feel like swearing, getting mad at God, or hurting someone, but the Holy Spirit can help us deal with our anger and trust God.**

We might lose control by indulging in too much of something we enjoy, such as TV or video games or chocolate, but the Holy Spirit reminds us that we need to honor God in everything we do.

COMMITMENT

Control Goals

Before class, make a sample of the "Control Freak" handout (p. 107).

Hold up the sample and say: **I have a little friend who can remind you that God wants us to be thoughtful and wise. His name is Control Freak.**

Distribute scissors, markers or crayons, and copies of the "Control Freak" handout (p. 107). Set out a tape dispenser. Point out the words that are scattered around Control Freak, and have volunteers read them aloud.

Say: **Circle the words that indicate danger areas in which you need to practice self-control. Then fold your handout in half the long way, and cut the jagged line from the center to the corner of the mouth.**

Show kids how to fold the lips back and forth on the dotted lines, then pull the lips forward as they fold the card closed. As they open and close the card, the lips will move as if Control Freak is talking. Show kids how to tape the neck of a balloon to the back of the card, then pull the balloon through the mouth so it looks like a tongue.

Say: **The balloon can remind you of how hard you worked for control during the Hot Air Escape challenge at the beginning of class. When you allow God's Holy Spirit to work in your heart, you don't have to fight for control all by yourself. The Holy Spirit will help you and remind you to do what honors God.**

And this silly little Control Freak can be your buddy. When you open and close your card, it looks like Control Freak is talking to you. Find a partner, and share what Control Freak might say to you. What danger areas did you circle? In what areas of your life do you need to work on self-control?

Pause as kids share. Then say: **Now tell your partner one "Control Goal" you'll set for yourself this week. It might be about limiting the amount of time you watch TV. It might be about watching your language more carefully. It might be about working at having a better attitude toward someone or toward a task that you have to do. Take a minute to think of and share a Control Goal right now.**

CLOSING

Fruit Roundup

When kids have shared their Control Goals, have them turn to the back of the handout, where Galatians 5:22-23 is printed.

Say: **This is it! We've worked through the whole list of the fruit of the Spirit. Does anyone have these verses memorized?** Allow volunteers to say Galatians 5:22-23 from memory. Then ask:

● **How can all these things happen in your life?** (They happen if you let the Holy Spirit work in your heart; you have to ask God to help you.)

Say: **God builds these characteristics into our lives as we open our hearts and ask the Holy Spirit to work in us. We can't achieve all these things on our own. That's why Jesus called the Holy Spirit a "helper."**

Say: **Let's celebrate by singing our fruit of the Spirit song.**

If kids are very familiar with the song, sing it in a circle. Let each student sing one word of the song. Point to students so they'll know when to sing.

> **The Fruit of the Spirit**
> *(to the tune of "Rock Around the Clock")*
>
> Love and joy.
> Love, joy, peace.
> In your heart may they increase.
> We're talking patience, kindness, goodness, too.
> And faithfulness to last your whole life through.
> Gentleness and self-control—
> The fruit God's Spirit grows in you!
> (Repeat)

Say: **Well done! I know you'll keep growing in the Lord, and I'll be watching for the fruit of the Spirit in each of your lives. Let's close with prayer.** Pray: **Lord Jesus, we thank you for sending the Holy Spirit to be our helper so that we can grow to be more and more like you. Help us keep our Control Goals this week so we can honor you in every area of our lives. In your name we pray, amen.**

Remind kids to take their Control Freaks with them as they leave.

GOSSIP VIDEO GAME ANGER

TV Eating UGLY TALK

"BUT THE FRUIT OF THE SPIRIT IS
LOVE, JOY, PEACE,
PATIENCE, KINDNESS,
GOODNESS,
FAITHFULNESS,
GENTLENESS
AND SELF-CONTROL"

(Galatians 5:22-23).

HERE'S THE GOAL:
STAY IN CONTROL!

11 Happy Harvest!

(A Lesson for Thanksgiving or Any Time)

TEACHER TIP

This lesson works well with an intergenerational class. You may wish to invite families to join you for this session.

LESSON AIM

To help kids understand that ★ we celebrate God's goodness.

OBJECTIVES

Kids will
- decorate baskets and make harvest treats to serve in them,
- learn about harvest in Bible times,
- complete a paper quilt block and offer thanks for God's blessings, and
- share the joy of harvest time with others.

YOU'LL NEED

- ❑ a popcorn popper
- ❑ a small microwave oven
- ❑ popcorn
- ❑ cinnamon
- ❑ sugar
- ❑ salt
- ❑ butter
- ❑ measuring cups and spoons
- ❑ large bowls and pans
- ❑ mixing spoons
- ❑ photocopies of the cinnamon popcorn recipe (p. 112)
- ❑ medium or large paper grocery bags
- ❑ curling ribbon or crepe paper streamers
- ❑ a large, round basket or tray
- ❑ a stalk of wheat, a jar of flour, and a loaf of bread (optional)
- ❑ balloons
- ❑ photocopies of the "Patchwork of Thanks" handout (p. 116)
- ❑ crayons or markers

❑ scissors
❑ tape
❑ a hole punch

Deuteronomy 8:1-18

For the people of Israel, harvest time meant days of intense work that culminated the growing season. The threats and hazards were many. Excessive rain or hail could ruin maturing crops. At various times in Israel's history, stronger neighbors swooped down and ruined or stole crops just as they were ready to be harvested. Crops were susceptible to various diseases, drought, and hot winds. Occasionally ravenous swarms of grasshoppers stripped fields clean. Given all these variables, a harvest safely accomplished was truly a sign of God's continued blessing.

The climate and soil of Israel typically allowed for three harvests. Wheat was planted in the fall and harvested in the spring. The Feast of Weeks celebrated the end of the wheat harvest, fifty days after Passover. Grape harvest began in summer and culminated in the Feast of Tabernacles in the fall. In the late summer and fall, as the grape harvest neared its end, dates, figs, and olives ripened.

God clearly meant for his people to celebrate at harvest time. Scripture speaks of it repeatedly: "Be joyful at your Feast—you, your sons and daughters, your menservants and maidservants, and the Levites, the aliens, the fatherless and the widows who live in your towns. For seven days celebrate the Feast to the Lord your God at the place the Lord will choose. For the Lord your God will bless you in all your harvest and in all the work of your hands, and your joy will be complete" (Deuteronomy 16:14-15). The joy mandated here is not based on the abundance of food, but in God's continued blessing on the land and its inhabitants. The people were to remember that when they were slaves in Egypt, God promised to bring them to a land flowing with milk and honey. Each harvest brought a reminder of that promise and of God's faithfulness.

Deuteronomy 26:1-2

God wants us to acknowledge and give thanks for the continuous stream of blessings he pours into our lives. Though our "first fruits" may not be agricultural in nature, we can still honor God with offerings and praises for the abundance we enjoy.

UNDERSTANDING YOUR KIDS

Thanksgiving is a terrific time for kids to focus on God. They aren't distracted by the anticipation of getting things. There are no Thanksgiving stockings or harvest bunnies that bring baskets of goodies. They don't make Thanksgiving lists, nor do they look for presents under a Thanksgiving tree. Somehow this joyful season has not been secularized and commercialized with expectations much beyond turkey and pumpkin pie. How refreshing!

Use this lesson to help kids see that God brings many kinds of blessings into our lives and that it pleases God when we celebrate his goodness.

The Lesson ATTENTION GRABBER

Cinnamon Harvest

If it's possible, set up a popcorn popper and a small microwave oven in your classroom for this lesson. If your situation doesn't allow that, plan to take kids to a kitchen.

Set up two work centers.

At a cinnamon popcorn center, set out the popcorn popper and microwave, sugar, cinnamon, salt, glass measuring cups and teaspoon measures. You'll also need large bowls or pans, mixing spoons, and photocopies of the cinnamon popcorn recipe (p. 112).

Set up a basket decorators center with paper grocery bags, a hole punch, and curling ribbon or crepe paper in harvest colors.

Say: **It's harvest time, and we're here to celebrate! I need cinnamon popcorn makers and basket decorators. The cinnamon popcorn makers will follow the recipe I've set out and use these ingredients to make yummy cinnamon popcorn to share. The basket decorators will use grocery bags and ribbons to make cool-looking baskets that we'll put the popcorn in when we take it to share with others.**

Put an adult, a teenage helper, or a reliable older child in charge of the cinnamon popcorn center. Explain exactly what setting of the microwave to use to melt the butter. (It must be a very low setting.) Emphasize that only kids who handle the ingredients carefully will be allowed to work in the cinnamon popcorn center. Plan to allow kids to make two or three batches so you'll have plenty of cinnamon popcorn to share later in the lesson.

Invite everyone to watch as you make one harvest basket at the basket decorators center. Cut off the top half of a grocery bag; then carefully fold the top down two inches to form a cuff. Pinch and crumple the top slightly to fold the cuff over once more; then smooth it out. Punch a hole through the cuff in the middle of each narrow side. Cut six thirty-inch lengths of curling ribbon. Fold three lengths in half, push the loop at the middle through one of the holes in the bag starting from the inside; then pull the ends through the loop and tighten. Repeat on the other side of the bag. Or cut six two-foot lengths of crepe paper. Twist three ends together, push them through a hole, knot them, and pull the knot tight against the hole. Repeat on the other side of the bag.

TEACHER TIP

If you don't have access to a microwave oven, bring the melted butter to class in covered glass jars. Kids can mix the rest of the ingredients right in the jars. You'll need to bring kitchen towels to wrap around the warm jars so kids can handle them safely.

Let kids choose the center where they'd like to work. Have plenty of bags and ribbon on hand so everyone who wishes to can make a harvest basket. If families are attending this class, encourage each family to make a harvest basket.

Allow everyone to take very small samples of the cinnamon popcorn as it's made. Allow about ten minutes for kids to work at the centers. Give a two-minute warning before you ask them to begin to clean up. Have kids set the baskets and cinnamon popcorn aside.

Say: **We celebrate God's goodness at harvest time, and our celebration has just begun. Let's find out more about the wonderful feasts and celebrations God planned for his people at harvest time.**

BIBLE STUDY

A Bible-Time Harvest (Deuteronomy 8:1-18)

Say: **Did you know that God actually instructed his people to throw a party at harvest time? That's right. God wanted his people to bring their offerings, give thanks, then have a wonderful time rejoicing and feasting together. Let's read what the Bible says about that.**

Have a volunteer look up and read aloud Deuteronomy 16:13-15.

Say: **God instructed his people to celebrate two harvest feasts—one in the spring, and one in the fall. You see, farmers planted grain in the fall— kind of like our winter wheat. It grew over the winter and ripened after the spring rains. Workers cut the wheat with scythes. A scythe had a sturdy handle and a long, curved blade. I need about four kids to be wheat.** Have four volunteers stand close together. Pretend to swing a scythe near their feet, then have them fall to the ground. Have them remain stiff and straight like a stalk of grain. **Several stalks of grain would fall with one skillful cut. Then another worker would bundle the grain into sheaves.** Roll the children together and pretend to tie them around the middle. **All the sheaves would be gathered onto donkeys or carts and carried to the village threshing floor.** Thank the "wheat children" and have them rejoin the group.

The threshing floor was a big, open space of hard-packed dirt. From the book of Ruth we know that landowners sometimes slept by their piles of grain to protect them from robbers. At the threshing floor, the grain would be spread out. Oxen would be hooked up to a heavy sledge that had pointed rocks or bits of iron attached to the underside. The oxen would drag the sledge over the grain to separate the heads from the stalks. Sometimes children would get to ride on the sledge to make it heavier.

Once the heads were separated from the stalks, the grain had to be *winnowed.* **That meant separating the chaff, the non-edible part, from the good kernels of grain. A harvester would pick up some stalks with a winnowing fork, which was kind of a cross between a pitchfork and a rake. He would toss the stalks into the air, and the heavier heads would fall first while the stalks blew away.**

Then the heads of grain would go into a basket. Pour several kernels

111

Cinnamon Popcorn

Makes 3 quarts (12 cups) of popcorn.

Pop enough popcorn kernels to measure 12 cups of popcorn.

In a large glass measuring cup, melt ½ cup butter.
Add ¼ cup sugar, ½ teaspoon cinnamon, and ¼ teaspoon salt.

Stir carefully until the sugar is nearly dissolved.

Pour the butter mixture over the popcorn and mix well.

(Optional: Bake in a large pan for 15 minutes at 300 degrees.)

Cinnamon Popcorn

Makes 3 quarts (12 cups) of popcorn.

Pop enough popcorn kernels to measure 12 cups of popcorn.

In a large glass measuring cup, melt ½ cup butter.
Add ¼ cup sugar, ½ teaspoon cinnamon, and ¼ teaspoon salt.

Stir carefully until the sugar is nearly dissolved.

Pour the butter mixture over the popcorn and mix well.

(Optional: Bake in a large pan for 15 minutes at 300 degrees.)

Cinnamon Popcorn

Makes 3 quarts (12 cups) of popcorn.

Pop enough popcorn kernels to measure 12 cups of popcorn.

In a large glass measuring cup, melt ½ cup butter.
Add ¼ cup sugar, ½ teaspoon cinnamon, and ¼ teaspoon salt.

Stir carefully until the sugar is nearly dissolved.

Pour the butter mixture over the popcorn and mix well.

(Optional: Bake in a large pan for 15 minutes at 300 degrees.)

of popcorn into a large, round basket. Toss the kernels into the air, and catch them again in the basket. **When they were tossed in the air, a slight wind would catch the chaff and blow it away, while the good kernels of grain would fall back into the basket.** Set the basket aside.

People with small fields might store the grain in clay jars. Wealthy farmers with lots of land stored it in barns. When it was time to make bread, the grain had to be ground into flour. It could be placed in a large stone bowl and ground with a smaller stone. Or it could be milled between two large stones. Then, finally, flour could be made into bread. Whew!

Ask:

● **Where does your bread come from?** (The store; the cupboard.)

Say: **Getting a piece of bread may seem like a simple thing to us. But when people in Bible times ate a piece of bread, they remembered plowing the field; planting the seeds; waiting during the long winter months; praying for rain in the spring; praying for good, dry weather for harvest; cutting the grain; bundling it; taking it to the threshing floor; winnowing it; grinding it into flour; and finally baking the bread. And when that process was over, they were ready to celebrate and give thanks!**

Those families who were able would go up to Jerusalem to celebrate the grain harvest at the Feast of Weeks. Everyone would take loaves of bread made from the new grain and give thanks at the Temple. Those who couldn't go to Jerusalem would celebrate and give thanks at the synagogues in their own villages.

The second harvest of the year was the grape harvest. That started in the summer and extended into early fall. Most grapes grew on hillsides above the villages, where it was cooler. The vineyards were separate from the other fields and often were far from the owners' houses. As the grapes ripened during the summer, families might move out by their vineyards and sleep there to protect their grapes. Some grapes were kept for drying and making raisins. The rest were crushed to make wine. And what a celebration that was! Let's blow up some balloons to represent bunches of grapes.

Allow each student to blow up a balloon and tie it off. Have everyone stand in a circle around the balloons. **The grapes were placed in a round, stone vat called a *wine press*. And villagers stomped on the grapes to squeeze out the juice that ran into another vat below. Let's stomp our grapes!** Lead kids in stomping the balloons until they've all popped.

You can imagine that they had a great time, just as we did! There was a lot of singing and dancing. The grape juice was poured into clay jars. And when that was done, the harvest season was complete.

Then everyone gathered offerings for the Lord and prepared for the Feast of Tabernacles. It was kind of like Thanksgiving and New Year's all rolled into one! Every family used branches to make little shelters in the streets and on the rooftops. They lived in these shelters for a week. You can imagine the festive atmosphere in the city with all the visitors bringing their offerings to the Temple, all the little shelters, and lots of good food to share. Merchants brought special things to sell because they knew the visitors would be in the city for just a short time. Uncles and aunts

TEACHER TIP

To illustrate the steps of the process you've just described, you may want to display a stalk or bundle of wheat, a small jar of whole-wheat flour, and a round loaf of bread or a piece of pita bread.

113

and cousins who rarely saw each other got to spend time together.

But the high point of the whole celebration was bringing offerings to the Temple and thanking God for blessing the year with a good harvest. Even though we can't travel to Jerusalem, we can have our own special harvest celebration right now. Let's find out how we can celebrate God's goodness.

LIFE APPLICATION

Patchwork of Thanks

Have a volunteer find and read aloud Deuteronomy 26:1-2a. Ask:
- **What are "first fruits"?** (The first and best part of the harvest.)
- **Since some of us don't have a harvest of fruit or vegetables, what can we offer thanks for?** (Our homes and cars; our jobs; our good health.)

Say: **We celebrate God's goodness at harvest time, and I have a unique way for us to offer our thanks. Our celebration will involve giving a basket of thanks to God.**

Distribute the crayons or markers, scissors, and the "Patchwork of Thanks" handout (p. 116). Have participants form groups of four. Place older participants in groups with nonreaders to help the younger ones complete their quilt blocks.

Say: **Cut out your quilt block on the heavy lines. Then answer the three questions on the quilt block. You may write or draw your answers, then share them with your group. When you've finished answering the questions and discussing your answers, fill in the triangles with flowers in one color. Then fill in the basket shape with the squiggles in another color. Use whatever colors you wish. Leave the top square and the two side triangles blank.**

Allow groups about ten minutes to work on their handouts and discuss what they're drawing and writing. Circulate among the groups to offer help and ideas as needed. Encourage everyone to give thoughtful answers to each question.

Give a two-minute warning before you ask everyone to clean up and put away the scissors and markers or crayons. Then gather everyone in a circle. Have kids place their finished quilt blocks on the floor in front of them. Invite kids to tell about the interesting things various people in their groups gave thanks for.

TEACHER TIP

You might want to take a photograph of the kids standing around the patchwork of thanks, then have a print made for each child.

COMMITMENT

A Wall of Thanks

After several kids have shared, say: **Remember how the Scripture we read earlier talked about bringing an offering in a basket? Now each of you has a basket to offer in thanks to the Lord. We'll celebrate God's goodness as we assemble our baskets into a beautiful patchwork of thanks.**

One by one, have groups tape their quilt blocks to a wall or table. Help them arrange the blocks in a solid cluster to give the impression of a quilt. As you arrange the quilt, have a good singer lead favorite praise songs.

Gather in front of the complete patchwork of thanks. If you wish, sing some lively songs with a Jewish theme, such as "It Is Good to Give Thanks" or "Jehovah Jireh." Then pray a prayer similar to this one: **Dear Lord, we offer you our thanks for the wonderful blessings represented on this wall. Thank you for giving us a good year. Thank you for the blessings we enjoy each day. Help us to remember that all these good things come from your hand. In Jesus' name we pray, amen.**

CLOSING

Celebrate!

Say: **Now it's time to share our joy with other folks here at church! In just a moment we'll form groups to distribute the cinnamon popcorn we made earlier. As you offer the popcorn, explain that we're celebrating God's goodness. Invite everyone to come and look at our patchwork of thanks and enjoy more cinnamon popcorn.**

Assign kids to groups. Designate one person in each group to carry a harvest basket of cinnamon popcorn. Explain that the other kids can invite everyone to visit the class and see the patchwork of thanks.

When visitors come to class, have kids point out their own quilt blocks and tell about the things they're thankful for. You may wish to leave the quilt on display for another week. If you have kids who won't be back, let them take their quilt blocks. Rearrange the remaining blocks to make a solid quilt.

Give everyone a copy of the cinnamon popcorn recipe to take home. Encourage participants to celebrate God's goodness each time they make it!

TEACHER TIP

If you're holding an intergenerational class, you might want to end with more harvest treats such as caramel apples or pumpkin bars or with a full-fledged potluck meal!

PATCHWORK OF THANKS

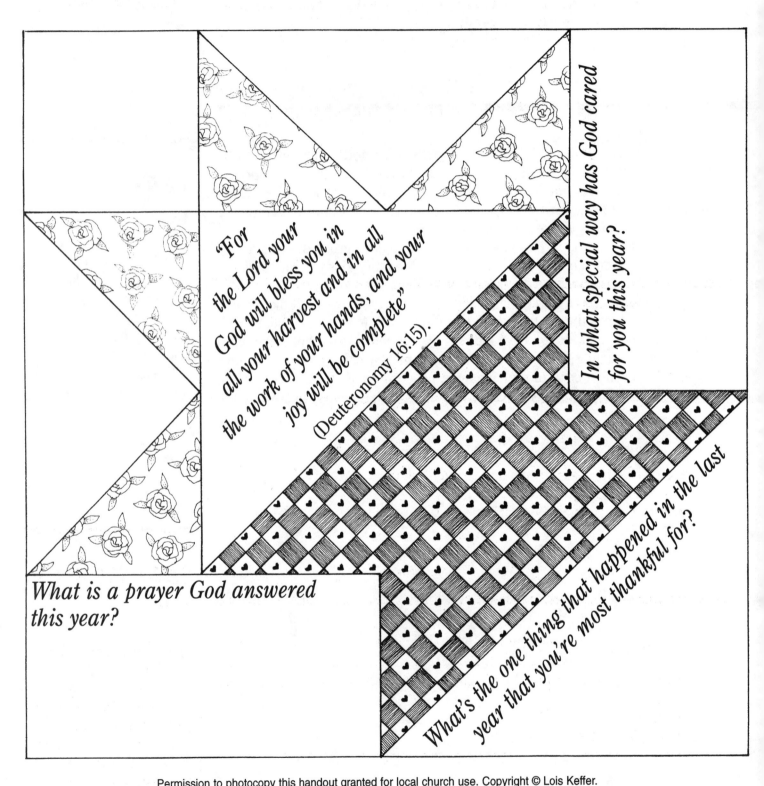

In what special way has God cared for you this year?

"For the Lord your God will bless you in all your harvest and in all the work of your hands, and your joy will be complete" (Deuteronomy 16:15).

What is a prayer God answered this year?

What's the one thing that happened in the last year that you're most thankful for?

Published in *Sunday School Specials 4* by Group Publishing, Inc., P.O. Box 481, Loveland, CO 80539.

God's Christmas Promise

12

(A Lesson for Christmas or for Christmas in July)

LESSON AIM

To help kids understand that ★ Jesus is the Savior God promised.

OBJECTIVES

Kids will
- play a game to learn why they need a savior,
- participate in an interactive Christmas story,
- create Christmas projects that remind them that Jesus is the Savior God promised, and
- have an opportunity to commit to telling others that Jesus is the Savior.

YOU'LL NEED

❑ treats
❑ materials for the Christmas learning centers of your choice:

❑ photocopies on green paper of the "Advent Holly Wreath" patterns (pp. 125-126)
❑ scissors
❑ red glitter glue

TEACHER TIP

This lesson works well with an intergenerational class. You may wish to invite families to join you for this session. Or you might consider using these ideas as the basis for a family Advent night.

❏ photocopies of the "Christmas Votive-Candle Holder" instructions (p. 127)
❏ clean tin cans filled with ice
❏ pencils
❏ hammers
❏ nails
❏ newspapers

❏ photocopies of the "Baby-in-a-Manger Treats" instructions (p. 128)
❏ a mixing bowl
❏ a jar of melted margarine
❏ measuring cups
❏ peanut butter
❏ marshmallow creme
❏ chow mein noodles
❏ a tablespoon measure
❏ large spoons
❏ small paper plates
❏ small pretzel logs
❏ orange circus peanut candies
❏ fruit leather

BIBLE BASIS

Luke 2:1-20

It's always a joy to come back to Christmas! No matter how many times we revisit the story, the wonder and joy of that miraculous birth wind themselves around our hearts. The wonder lies in the great paradoxes that we can only begin to comprehend. The voice that once spoke our world into being confines itself to the coos and cries of a newborn. The hand that would someday be pierced for us now clings fiercely to a young mother. Simple shepherds who expected nothing more than a long night with their sheep on a chilly hillside now answer an angelic summons to look in the face of deity. The Lord who possesses all the riches of heaven empties himself to enter a humble family. Men renowned for their wisdom travel a great distance to pay homage to a wordless infant whose wisdom is infinitely greater than theirs.

It's all so surprising, this plan of salvation that God set in motion two thousand years ago. It's so unlike how we would have done it, so unscientific, so downright off-the-wall! Brilliant minds of the secular world rebel at the audacious simplicity of God's plan—to send a holy child who would live a perfect life, die a sacrificial death, then rise to conquer Satan's power and offer eternal life to those whose faith is bold enough to believe him.

The joy is in the sweet realization that it's all true—that this infant Savior was born for you!

Isaiah 7:14; 9:6-7; 11:1-2

For hundreds of years before Jesus' birth, prophets had been seeing God-given visions of his kingdom that was to come. The details of his birth and life and death are irrefutably written in Old Testament Scripture. Anyone who truly desires to investigate and compare prophecy to fulfillment can see and believe.

UNDERSTANDING YOUR KIDS

Schoolchildren learn to deal in cold, hard facts. They learn to observe and apply the scientific method—to create and test theories and hypotheses and determine if an experiment will bring the same results twice. Faith may be dismissed as superstition and old wives' tales. Or it may be accepted—there are many brilliant scientists and physicists who are so awed by the wonder of the universe they study that faith in an infinitely wise, powerful God is the only logical response.

It feels really terrific to point to Old Testament Scriptures that foretell with pinpoint accuracy important details of Jesus' birth, life, death, and resurrection. Your kids can direct skeptics of any age to these Scriptures and say, "You want proof? *Here's proof!*" Use this lesson to help kids see that Old Testament prophecies help us understand that baby Jesus truly is the Savior God promised.

ATTENTION GRABBER The Lesson

No Perfect People

Bring delicious-looking treats to class on a festive Christmas plate or tray. Place the treats where they'll be sure to be noticed as everyone arrives. If kids ask when they'll be allowed to eat the treats, tell them they'll find out in a few minutes.

Hold up the plate of treats and say: **Several of you have noticed these treats. They do look good, don't they? And I'd just love to share them with you. But you're going to have to qualify for them. You see, these are such perfectly wonderful treats that I can share them only with perfect people.**

Please line up facing me with the smallest person in front and the tallest person in back.

When everyone has lined up, approach the first child and ask:

● **Have you ever done anything you shouldn't do?**

When that child answers, "yes," say: **I'm sorry, I guess I can't give you a treat. You'll have to go sit down.** Ask the rest of the kids in line any combination of these questions.

● **Have you ever said anything you shouldn't say?**
● **Have you ever disobeyed a parent?**
● **Have you ever hurt someone's feelings?**

119

● **Have you ever gotten angry when you shouldn't have?**

One by one, dismiss everyone in line. When you're left holding the treats, say: **You know what? I've done all of those things too. I guess I can't have any of these treats either.**

Set the plate of treats down and go sit with the others. Don't give any indication of what's going to happen next until kids grow restless and start to question you. Then say: **Well, I'm not sure what to do. My instructions were that I could share those treats only with perfect people. But none of us is perfect. We've all blown it sometime in our lives. What are we going to do?**

Let kids offer suggestions until someone mentions that's why Jesus came. If no one offers that suggestion, bring it up yourself. Say: **No one is perfect. That's why God sent Jesus into the world. Do you remember the story of Creation?** Ask:

● **Who were the very first people God made?** (Adam and Eve.)

● **What did they do wrong?** (They ate fruit from the tree God had said not to eat from.)

Say: **Adam and Eve sinned and disobeyed God. And ever since, every person who has lived has sinned and disobeyed God.** Hold up the plate of treats. **God has something wonderful to share with us—much more wonderful than these treats! It's called heaven.** Ask:

● **Who can tell me about heaven?** (Jesus is there; the streets are made of gold; we'll live there forever; we'll be very happy there.)

● **But there's no sin in heaven, so if we've all sinned, how can we go there?** (We need Jesus to forgive our sins.)

Say: **God knew that people could never be perfect. So long ago, he promised to send a Savior who would take away their sins. God's prophets began writing about Jesus hundreds of years before he was born. Let's read some of the things they wrote.**

Have volunteers look up and read Isaiah 7:14; 9:6-7.

Say: **The prophet Isaiah wrote those words about Jesus, the Savior God would send into the world hundreds of years later. Listen to something else Isaiah wrote: "Comfort, comfort, my people, says your God. Speak tenderly to Jerusalem, and proclaim to her that her hard service has been completed, that her sin has been paid for"** (Isaiah 40:1-2a).

Distribute the treats as you say: **You're not perfect, and I'm not perfect. So God sent a Savior to pay for our sins. Jesus is the Savior God promised. Because Jesus came, God can share heaven with us someday. Let's celebrate the story of his birth in a fun and different way.**

BIBLE STUDY

The Savior's Birth

Say: **You're going to help me tell the Christmas story today by responding to certain words. Whenever I say "angel," you say, "Prrrang!"— a kind of special effects noise for when something just appears out of**

120

nowhere. At the same time, make your fingers "twinkle" by wiggling them quickly around your face. Have kids try that.

Whenever I say "Mary," girls respond by fanning your hands around your face and saying in a sweet, soft voice, "highly favored." Mary. Lead girls in responding.

Whenever I say "Joseph," boys respond by saying in a deep voice, "a good man!" Joseph. Lead boys in responding.

Whenever I say "baby," everyone say, "our Savior and king." Baby. Lead everyone in responding.

Whenever I say, "shepherds," everyone say, "sheep-sheep-sheep!" Shepherds. Lead kids in saying, "sheep-sheep-sheep!"

Give the various cue words in random order to make sure everyone knows the responses. Then begin the story.

Long, long ago in the town of Nazareth there lived a kind carpenter named *Joseph*. He was engaged to a lovely young woman named *Mary*, who loved God with all her heart.

One day a most unusual visitor came to see *Mary*. It was the *angel* Gabriel. He said, "Greetings, you who are highly favored. The Lord is with you."

Mary was surprised and troubled. Why was an *angel* visiting her? And what did his greeting mean? The *angel* could see that she was confused and fearful. He said, "Don't be afraid. God is pleased with you. You will have a *baby,* and you are to name him Jesus. He will be great—the Son of the Most High God. The Lord will give him the throne of his ancestor David and his kingdom will never end."

Mary didn't know what to think! "But how can this be since I'm not married?" she asked.

The *angel* explained, "Your *baby* will come from God."

"I am willing to do whatever the Lord wants," she responded. "May everything you said come true."

When *Joseph* discovered that *Mary* was going to have a baby, he decided not to marry her after all. But then the *angel* appeared to him in a dream and told him to go ahead and get married because the *baby* was from God.

Not long after that, the Roman government put out a decree for all the people to go to their hometowns to be taxed. *Joseph's* hometown was Bethlehem. It was a ninety-mile trip from Nazareth to Bethlehem—a distance that took about five days to walk. Let's walk around the room once for each day they had to travel. Lead everyone around the room (or around a larger area) five times; then gather kids in a group again.

That was quite a difficult trip for a young woman who was expecting a *baby*.

When *Joseph* and *Mary* arrived in Bethlehem, the little village was crammed with people! Everyone stand together in the smallest possible space you can. Pause as everyone clumps together. Everything was crowded; people were tired and probably crabby! Turn to the people next to you and say, "Crabbity-crabbity-crab!" Lead kids in doing this.

There was no place to stay—not a single room in the whole town. Finally, *Joseph* led *Mary* to a quiet stable. It may have been in a cave on a hillside above the town. And there she gave birth to a *baby* boy. She named him Jesus. Because there was no bed, she wrapped little Jesus in cloths and laid him in a manger full of hay.

On a hillside nearby, *shepherds* were watching over their flocks. The night was dark and quiet. Suddenly a blinding light filled the sky, and an *angel* said, "Don't be afraid. I bring you good news that will bring joy to everyone. Today in the town of David a Savior has been born for you. He is Christ the Lord. This is how you'll find him—he'll be wrapped in cloths and lying in a manger."

Then the *angel* was joined by so many other *angels* that they nearly filled the night sky. They praised God, saying, "Glory to God in the highest and peace on earth to those who please him." Then the sky grew dark and quiet again.

The *shepherds* rushed off to Bethlehem and found *baby* Jesus in the manger, just as the *angel* had said. After they had worshipped the Christ child, the *shepherds* rushed off to tell everyone about the wonderful things that had happened.

Have kids give themselves a round of applause for their participation in the story. Then say: **One of the most amazing things about Jesus' birth is how much Old Testament Scriptures told about it. Just before the story, we read some passages from the book of Isaiah, which was written about seven hundred years before Jesus' birth.** You may want to reread Isaiah 7:14; 9:6-7. Ask:

● **What did Isaiah tell us about Jesus' birth?** (That Jesus' mother would be a virgin; that Jesus would be the Savior; that Jesus would be related to David.)

Say: **We also find an interesting fact about Jesus' birth in the book by the prophet Micah, who lived at the same time as Isaiah.** Look up and read Micah 5:2. Then ask:

● **What does that prophecy tell about Jesus' birth?** (That Jesus would come from Bethlehem.)

Before class, make a sample of the Advent holly wreath from the patterns on pages 125-126. Hold up the Advent wreath and say: **In just a few moments, we'll be doing some Christmas projects. One of the choices is an Advent wreath like this one. Each section of the wreath has two Scripture passages printed on it. One is from an Old Testament prophecy about Jesus' birth. The second passage is from the New Testament. It tells how that prophecy came true.**

Set the wreath aside and continue: **Seeing all the prophecy that came true at Jesus' birth helps us believe that Jesus is the Savior God promised. When we study the rest of Jesus' life, we find even more connections with prophecies from the Old Testament. And we, like the shepherds, can tell others these wonderful things about Jesus.**

Now let's have fun making some Christmas projects that remind us that Jesus is the Savior God promised.

Christmas Learning Centers

Choose one, two, or all three of these Christmas learning-center ideas. Each is easy to prepare and fun for kids as well as adults. And each center allows kids to actively explore the important truth that Jesus is the Savior God promised.

If you have time, let kids do all the projects. If time is limited, offer photocopies of the instructions from each center for kids to take home.

● **Advent Holly Wreath**—Photocopy the "Advent Holly Wreath" patterns (pp. 125-126) onto green paper. You'll need one set of patterns for each person who chooses this project. Set out the patterns, scissors, and red glitter glue. Kids will cut out the four sections of the pattern and add red glitter glue to the holly berries. Then they'll attach the four sections to form a ring. This craft complements the Christmas Votive-Candle Holder below that can be placed in the center of the wreath as the Christ candle.

● **Christmas Votive-Candle Holder**—Before class, clean several small tin cans, and remove the labels. Fill the cans with water, and freeze them. Keep them frozen until class time by storing them in the church freezer or in a cooler. Set out hammers, nails, newspapers, the ice-filled cans, and a copy of the "Christmas Votive-Candle Holder" instructions (p. 127). Kids will hammer cross designs into the cans, remove the ice, and insert votive candles.

● **Baby-in-a-Manger Treats**—Set out photocopies of the "Baby-in-a-Manger Treats" instructions (p. 128), small paper plates, small pretzel logs, marshmallow creme, peanut butter, chow mein noodles, a jar of melted margarine, measuring cups, a tablespoon measure, a mixing bowl, and a large spoon. You'll also need orange circus peanut candies and a package of rolled fruit leather such as Fruit Roll-Ups. Kids will stir together a delicious "hay" mixture and put it on a plate, then press pretzels into the hay to form a manger. They'll place a circus peanut "baby" on top after wrapping it with fruit leather to represent swaddling clothes. One recipe will make enough of the hay mixture for about ten students.

Announce when there are five minutes of working time left, then two minutes, then one. When you call time, have participants gather their projects and sit in a circle. Tell students to place their crafts on the floor behind them.

TEACHER TIP

It's a good idea to prepare a sample of each of the projects to show to the kids. You may want to recruit a teenage or adult helper to make the samples and help out during class.

COMMITMENT

Share the Savior

Say: **I'd like you to think for a moment about someone who doesn't know that Jesus is the Savior God promised.**

Pause as students think. Then say: **Now talk with someone sitting near you about a way you might tell that person about the importance of Jesus' birth. Tell your partner how you could share the good news about**

Jesus with that person.

After partners have talked, ask volunteers to share their plans for telling someone about Jesus.

CLOSING

Christmas Thanks

Have kids hold their projects as you close with a prayer similar to this one: **Dear Jesus, thank you for coming to earth to be our Savior. Thank you for the joy that this special season brings to us because your coming means that we can look forward to being with you in heaven someday. Please help us tell others that you are the Savior God promised. In your name we pray, amen.**

ADVENT HOLLY WREATH 1

Cut around the outside of both sections; then cut the two slits in each section. Fasten these two sections together at the slits; then add the two sections from "Advent Holly Wreath 2" to form a circle. If you wish, add red glitter glue to the holly berries. At home, place a candle in a holder in the center of the wreath.

The first Scripture passage in each section gives an Old Testament prophecy about Jesus' birth; the second passage is from the New Testament and tells how the prophecy came true. Plan to read these Scriptures aloud with your family.

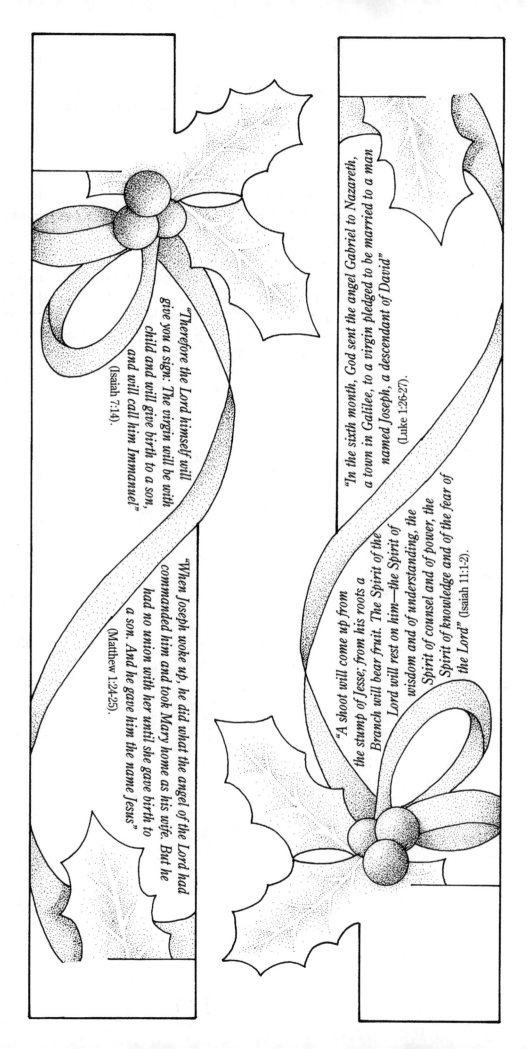

"Therefore the Lord himself will give you a sign: The virgin will be with child and will give birth to a son, and will call him Immanuel" (Isaiah 7:14).

"When Joseph woke up, he did what the angel of the Lord had commanded him and took Mary home as his wife. But he had no union with her until she gave birth to a son. And he gave him the name Jesus" (Matthew 1:24-25).

"In the sixth month, God sent the angel Gabriel to Nazareth, a town in Galilee, to a virgin pledged to be married to a man named Joseph, a descendant of David" (Luke 1:26-27).

"A shoot will come up from the stump of Jesse; from his roots a Branch will bear fruit. The Spirit of the Lord will rest on him—the Spirit of wisdom and of understanding, the Spirit of counsel and of power, the Spirit of knowledge and of the fear of the Lord" (Isaiah 11:1-2).

ADVENT HOLLY WREATH 2

Cut around the outside of both sections; then cut the two slits in each section. Fasten these two sections together at the slits; then add the two sections from "Advent Holly Wreath 2" to form a circle. If you wish, add red glitter glue to the holly berries. At home, place a candle in a holder in the center of the wreath.

The first Scripture passage in each section gives an Old Testament prophecy about Jesus' birth; the second passage is from the New Testament and tells how the prophecy came true. Plan to read these Scriptures aloud with your family.

"For to us a child is born, to us a son is given, and the government will be on his shoulders. And he will be called Wonderful Counselor, Mighty God, Everlasting Father, Prince of Peace. Of the increase of his government and peace there will be no end. He will reign on David's throne and over his kingdom" (Isaiah 9:6-7).

"You will be with child and give birth to a son, and you are to give him the name Jesus. He will be great and will be called the Son of the Most High. The Lord God will give him the throne of his father David" (Luke 1:31-32).

"Jesus was born in Bethlehem in Judea, during the time of King Herod" (Matthew 2:1).

"But you, Bethlehem Ephrathah, though you are small among the clans of Judah, out of you will come for me one who will be ruler over Israel, whose origins are from of old, from ancient times" (Micah 5:2).

CHRISTMAS VOTIVE CANDLE HOLDER

1. Use pencil dots to mark cross patterns on both sides of the ice-filled tin can. Make the dots about a half-inch apart.

2. Find a partner. Have your partner hold the can with several thicknesses of newspaper.

3. Use a hammer and nail to gently punch a hole through each dot in your pattern. *Tap very lightly with the hammer.* It does not take much force to punch through the can.

4. Hold the can upside down under warm water until the ice falls out.

5. At home, place a votive candle in your can. The light from the candle will shine through the holes and make the crosses glow!

baby-in-a-manger treats

1. Work together with other kids to make the following recipe for "hay."

   In a mixing bowl, blend:

   2 tablespoons melted margarine

   1 7-ounce jar marshmallow creme

   ¼ cup peanut butter

   Stir in 3 cups chow mein noodles.

2. Place a mound of hay on the center of a small paper plate.

3. Take twelve small pretzel sticks. Build them log-cabin style around the mound of hay; then press the hay against the pretzels to help them hold together. Now you have a manger!

4. Tear a piece of fruit leather. Wrap it around a circus peanut candy as you would wrap a blanket around a baby.

5. Place the circus peanut candy in the center of the manger to represent baby Jesus.

Here Comes The Bride!

(A Lesson for Valentine's Day or Any Day)

13

LESSON AIM

To help kids understand that ★ God wants us to be helpful and kind even when no one else is watching.

OBJECTIVES

Kids will
- play a game and guess who's being affirmed,
- hear how a young woman's act of kindness caused Abraham's servant to choose her for Isaac's bride,
- create projects that emphasize friendship and kindness, and
- plan ways to be helpful and kind to people they don't usually notice.

YOU'LL NEED

- ❏ slips of paper
- ❏ pencils
- ❏ a basket
- ❏ a bottle of bubbles
- ❏ a photocopy of the "Eliezer's Journey" script (pp. 134-135)
- ❏ a costume for Eliezer—a robe, sandals, towels, neckties
- ❏ fiberfill or quilt batting for a beard, double-sided tape (optional)
- ❏ materials for the learning centers of your choice:

  - ❏ photocopies of the "Friendship Bracelets" instructions (p. 138)
  - ❏ scissors
  - ❏ leather shoelaces or heavy jute twine
  - ❏ assorted clay and plastic beads

TEACHER TIP

This lesson works well with an intergenerational class. You may wish to invite families to join you for this session.

129

- ❑ photocopies on red and pink paper of the "Folded Valentine Notes" pattern (p. 139)
- ❑ scissors
- ❑ markers
- ❑ glitter glue, rubber stamps and stamp pads, stickers (optional)

- ❑ photocopies of the "Masterpiece Cookies" instructions (p. 140)
- ❑ plain sugar cookies (homemade or from the store)
- ❑ canned frosting
- ❑ paper plates
- ❑ cinnamon hearts
- ❑ small gumdrops
- ❑ skinny licorice whips
- ❑ colorful sprinkles
- ❑ plastic knives
- ❑ sandwich bags

BIBLE BASIS

Genesis 24:1-67

When Abraham grew old, he began to be concerned about finding the right wife for his son, Isaac. Determined not to have Isaac marry a local Canaanite woman who would have come from a background of idol worship, Abraham sent a trusted servant back to Haran to find a woman from his own family. (This servant may have been Eliezer, who is mentioned in Genesis 15:2 as the probable recipient of Abraham's wealth if he were to die without a child of his own.)

The servant loaded ten camels with supplies and gifts and took off on the long trip. As the servant neared the town where Abraham's relatives lived, he paused and prayed for God's help and blessing in identifying the young woman who would marry Isaac. Before he even finished praying, Rebekah came to the well! When the servant asked her for a drink, she gave it, then graciously offered to draw water for his camels as well. Her act of kindness was exactly the sign the servant had prayed for!

Rebekah readily agreed to travel back to Canaan and marry her unknown cousin. And so she came to take her place in history as an ancestress of Christ. It was Rebekah's helpfulness to a stranger that helped identify her as God's choice to become Isaac's wife. Though it was common courtesy to offer a drink to a thirsty traveler, Rebekah went beyond the expected when she offered to provide as much water as the camels would drink. And she did it with no expectation of reward—she was completely unaware of the servant's identity and the rich gifts he was about to offer.

Matthew 25:34-40

Expectations for giving and receiving hospitality in Bible times were higher than most of us today would enjoy dealing with. Sharing the resources of the home was a binding obligation. But Jesus gave new meaning to offering the basic necessities of food, drink, and clothing when he said, "Whatever you did for one of the least of these brothers of mine, you did for me" (Matthew 25:40). We Christians today would do well to go out of our way to offer help and kindness to those who usually escape our notice.

UNDERSTANDING YOUR KIDS

When it comes to being helpful and kind, kids can be motivated more by self-interest than intrinsic goodness. If someone they want to impress is watching, they'll bend over backward to help. What greater honor can there be than to do an errand for the teacher? But when children have an opportunity to be helpful to someone who's not important to them, when no one's watching, it may be more difficult to find the motivation to act.

Use this lesson to teach kids that their small acts of helpfulness and caring are important to God.

ATTENTION GRABBER The Lesson

Bubbles of Kindness

As kids arrive, have them write their names on slips of paper and drop them into a basket. Then form pairs, matching younger children with older ones. New children to the class should be placed with partners who know everyone else.

Have partners sit facing each other, next to other pairs, forming a double circle. Pass the basket, and have everyone draw a name. If kids draw their own names or their partners' names, have them put the slips back and draw again. When everyone has drawn a name, say: **Please keep the names you have a secret until I tell you how and when to reveal them. You're going to say something kind about the person whose name you're holding—but you're not going to say who it is. You and your partner can work together to finish this sentence: "The thing I really like about this person is..." And you need to say something more than "He's nice" or "She's sweet." You might say, "The thing I really like about this person is that this person is always friendly and helpful," or "that this person always says something funny and cheers everyone up."**

Hold up a bottle of bubbles. **When I call on you to tell about the person whose name you've drawn, I'll hand you this bottle of bubbles. You'll tell about the person; then the rest of us will try to guess who you were talking about. When we guess the right person, you'll go to that person and blow bubbles over his or her head. Then you'll hand that person the bottle of bubbles, and he or she will be the next to talk.**

131

Here's an important rule: **In this game we'll say only good things about people—things that will make us all feel good. OK—go to a quiet spot with your partner. I'll give you two minutes to plan what you're going to say.**

Let partners scatter around the room to plan their affirmations. Circulate among partners to make sure everyone comes up with something positive and complimentary. After two minutes, call time and have everyone sit in a circle. Give the bottle of bubbles to an outgoing child to begin. When the group guesses the identity of the affirmed person, have the first child blow bubbles over his or her head, then pass the bubbles on. Continue until everyone has shared an affirmation. Then take the bottle of bubbles, and ask:

● **What was it like to hear nice things without knowing who they were about?** (Cool—I kept wondering if it was about me; it was fun to guess the person.)

● **How often do you go out of your way to say nice things to people?** (Not very often; I usually try to say nice things to my friends.)

● **Do you ever try to be nice to people you don't even know? Explain.** (Yes, I say "hi" to kids at school even if I don't know them; our family helps pay for food for a child in another country; I'm always polite to people at the store.)

Say: **It's easy to be kind and caring to people we know and like in a situation like this one where everyone is watching. And we sometimes go out of our way to be helpful to teachers or other leaders. But the Bible teaches us that it's important to be kind to people who don't seem to be especially important—people we may not even know. God wants us to be helpful and kind even when no one else is watching. Today's Bible story is about a young woman who did just that, and she became part of one of the greatest and most famous families of all time.**

BIBLE STUDY

Eliezer's Journey

Before class, arrange for an older man to visit your class in the role of Eliezer. Give him a photocopy of the script, "Eliezer's Journey" (pp. 134-135). Have him create a Bible-time costume from a bathrobe and sandals. Suggest a towel for a headpiece and strips of fabric or old neckties for a belt and a headband.

If you're planning an intergenerational class, choose one of the men who's present to play Eliezer. Make sure you choose someone who's comfortable reading a script in front of a group. Give him the script at the start of class so he can quickly read over it. When it's time for the story, kids will love helping to dress him in an improvised costume. If he's beardless, let kids use some quilt batting or fiberfill and double-sided tape to help him grow a beard right on the spot!

Tell your helper whether you'll sing "Father Abraham" as part of the story—it's mentioned in an optional section of the script.

Introduce him by saying: **I'm glad to tell you that we have a fascinating guest speaker today. He'll be telling you the Bible story. His name is Eliezer** (el-ih-EE-zur)**, and he is the most trusted servant of Abraham.**

Eliezer was almost like a son to Abraham...but I'll let *him* tell the story. So let's give a hearty welcome to Eliezer!

Lead kids in clapping and cheering; then encourage them to be attentive listeners.

After Eliezer finishes his story, have everyone give your helper a big round of applause. Then ask:

● **How would you like to have your mom or dad or uncle pick out a husband or wife for you?** (Yuck!; no way; I'm never getting married.)

● **What qualities was Eliezer hoping to find in a wife for Isaac?** (Someone who was kind and helpful; someone nice.)

● **How did Eliezer know for sure that Rebekah was the one God had chosen for Isaac?** (Because he prayed; because she gave him a drink and gave water for all of his camels, too.)

● **How many of you have ever been camping and had to carry water to your campsite? What's that like?** (It's hard; it's really heavy; you have to make more than one trip to get enough water for everybody.)

● **What do you think it would be like if you had to carry water in a heavy clay jar?** (I'm not sure; it would be really heavy.)

● **Why do you think Rebekah was helpful to a complete stranger?** (She was just a kind person; she wanted to be helpful.)

Say: **God wants us to be helpful and kind even when no one else is watching. Rebekah was helpful to Abraham's servant and was chosen to be one of the most famous brides in the Bible. But her actions showed that she would have been helpful and kind even if there had been no reward at all. Because she married into Abraham's family, she became Jesus' great-great-great-great...well, I don't know exactly how many "greats" there are...grandmother.**

Jesus was born about two thousand years after Abraham and Isaac. And he taught how important it is to show kindness to all people. Let's read Jesus' words in Matthew 25:34-40. Have a volunteer look up and read those verses aloud. Then ask:

● **What did Jesus mean by "the least of these brothers of mine"?** (People who aren't important; poor people.)

● **Who are the "least of these" in our world today?** (People in poor countries; people who live on the street; people who are unpopular.)

LIFE APPLICATION

Valentine Learning Centers

Say: **On Valentine's Day, we usually go out of our way to be caring and kind to people who are important to us.** Ask:

● **Who do you usually do nice things for on Valentine's Day?** (My mom and dad; my teacher; my good friends.)

Say: **This Valentine's Day I'd like to challenge you to be helpful and kind to someone who isn't expecting it, just as Rebekah was. Let's have**

Eliezer's Journey

A wife! I had to find a wife! Not for me, mind you, but for my master's son, Isaac. I'm sure you've heard of my master. He's one of the most famous people in the Bible. His name is Abraham.

[*Optional:* You know that song about Father Abraham? Would you like to sing it right now? Let's do! I think this nice person right here will help lead it.]

Abraham waited years and years and years for the son God had promised. In fact, he was one hundred years old when Isaac was born, and Sarah, his wife, was over ninety! When the time finally came to choose a wife for Isaac, Abraham needed my help. In my day, young men and women didn't go on dates or send Valentines or anything like that. Their parents decided who they would marry. I think that's a good idea, don't you?

So one day Abraham called me in and said, "Eliezer, I want you to make me a promise. It's time to choose a wife for Isaac, but I don't want a Canaanite woman from around here. I want you to go back to my home country of Haran, far to the north, and choose a wife for Isaac from my own people."

You see, the Canaanites who lived around us were idol worshippers. Abraham wanted Isaac's wife to be someone who would love God. Abraham also wanted me to promise not to take Isaac back to the old country. He knew that God had promised to make a new nation right here in Canaan.

Let me tell you, that was a lot to promise! But Abraham assured me that an angel would go before me and help me choose a wife for Isaac. So I agreed. I loaded up ten camels with supplies and all kinds of wonderful gifts for the bride-to-be. And I took off on a monthlong journey of more than six hundred miles back to Haran, the land we had left so long ago.

When I got there, I prayed like crazy that God would let me know which was the right young woman. As I came to the town where Abraham's family lived, it was near sunset, and the young women were coming out to the well to draw water during the cool of the day. I prayed, "God, I'm standing here by this spring, and all the young women of the town are coming. When I ask a girl for a drink from her water jar, please let her say, 'Drink, and I'll draw water for your camels, too.' Then I'll know that she's the one for Isaac."

Just then a very lovely young lady came to the well. I rushed to catch up with her.

"Please give me a little water from your jar," I said.

"Please help yourself," she answered, "and I'll draw water for your camels, too, until they've all had enough to drink."

The Lord be praised! She answered just as I had prayed. She was so very kind to offer to draw so much water for a stranger like me, for her water jar was heavy, and my camels were thirsty. This was just the kind of young woman who would make a wonderful wife for Isaac!

Her name was Rebekah. I asked about her family and discovered that she was related to Abraham. Her family invited me to have dinner and spend the night with them. I gave Rebekah beautiful gold jewelry and gifts from my master. Then she agreed to go back to Canaan with me and marry Isaac. God be praised!

We made the long journey back to Canaan, and Isaac came out to meet us. It was love at first sight! My master, Abraham, was so pleased to hear how God had helped me find Rebekah because of her act of kindness.

some fun with Valentine projects; then let's plan how we can use them to surprise someone.

Choose one, two, or all three of these Valentine learning center ideas. Or add or substitute favorite crafts and activities of your own.

Plan to do a sample of each item before class, or recruit a friend to make samples for you. Let kids explore the centers and choose what they'd like to make. If you have time, let them do all the projects. If time is limited, offer photocopies of the instructions from each center for kids to take home.

● **Friendship Bracelets**—This project is super simple, but kids love it! Kids will cut and knot lengths of leather shoelace or heavy jute twine. Friends will add clay or plastic beads between the knots. Then the ends will be tied together to form a bracelet. Set out copies of the "Friendship Bracelets" instructions (p. 138), leather laces or jute twine, a variety of clay and plastic beads, and sharp scissors.

● **Folded Valentine Notes**—Participants will cut and fold clever notes that form their own envelopes with heart-shaped flaps. A heart insert provides writing space for promise coupons or messages of kindness and encouragement. A verse about God's love is printed on each note. The notes may be decorated or sent as is. Participants may want to make more than one note, so be sure to make plenty of copies of the pattern. Set out copies of the "Folded Valentine Notes" pattern (p. 139) on red and pink paper, scissors, and decorating items of your choice such as rubber stamps and stamp pads, stickers, markers, and glitter glue.

● **Masterpiece Cookies**—Using canned frosting and candy decorations, kids will transform plain sugar cookies (homemade or from the store) into glittering valentine masterpieces. Make sure each person makes at least two cookies—one to eat and one to share. Set out photocopies of the "Masterpiece Cookies" instructions (p. 140), plastic knives, paper plates, canned frosting, sugar cookies, sandwich bags, and your choice of decorations such as cinnamon hearts, small gumdrops, skinny licorice whips, and colorful sprinkles.

Give kids a five-minute warning before it's time to clean up. Then give two-minute and one-minute warnings. After everyone has helped clean up, have kids gather in a circle with their projects on the floor behind them.

COMMITMENT

The Least of These

Say: **Form trios.** (It's fine to have one or two groups of four if that's the way your numbers work out.) Have trios discuss the following questions. Pause after each question to allow for discussion time.

● **When has someone you didn't know done something helpful and**

kind for you? (A man stopped to help us change a flat tire; a neighbor helped me when I fell off my bike.)

● **Why is it important to God that we're helpful and kind, even when no one else is watching?** (Because God sees us even if no one else does; because that's how we show God's love.)

● **Who is someone you see from time to time who is like the "least of these" Jesus talks about in Matthew 25?** (A kid at school who doesn't have any friends; an older man who comes to our church.)

● **How could you use something you made or learned today to be helpful and kind to that person?** (I could share a cookie with him; I could give her a note saying I'd like to be friends.)

After trios have discussed the last question, call everyone together and say: **I'd like to hear about some of the interesting answers you came up with in your trios.**

Allow several participants to share.

CLOSING

Kindly Pop My Bubble

Say: **God wants us to be helpful and kind, even when no one else is watching. Remember, even if no one else is watching, Jesus is. Jesus told us that when we do something kind for even the most unimportant person, it's like doing it for him. I hope you'll think about that this week when you see an older person who's having a difficult time getting around, when you see a child who's frightened or confused, or when an unpopular person at school is sitting all alone in the lunchroom.**

Valentine's Day is a good time to begin a habit of helpfulness and kindness that lasts all year! I'm going to blow some bubbles in the air. I'd like you to try to pop them all before they hit the ground. Each time you pop a bubble, shout out one kind, helpful thing you'll do this week. Ready? Here we go!

Blow several strong puffs of bubbles in different directions. If you have adults in your class, make sure you aim some of the bubbles toward them! Then gather everyone for prayer.

Pray: **Dear Lord, please help us scatter acts of kindness all around us this week. Help us to remember that you want us to be helpful and kind even when no one else is watching, because *you're* always watching. Help us show friendship in your name to people we usually don't even notice. In Jesus' name, amen.**

Friendship Bracelets

1. Cut a twelve-inch length of a leather shoelace or jute twine.

2. Tie a knot three inches from one end.

3. Ask a friend to slide a bead on the other end. Push the bead clear up to the knot.

4. Have friends add as many beads as you like. Tie more knots between the beads wherever you'd like them.

5. Drape the bracelet comfortably around your wrist. Have a friend tie the two ends together. Make sure the bracelet is loose enough to slide on and off easily.

6. Trim the two ends to the same length.

7. Help other friends make their bracelets!

Folded Valentine Notes

Cut out the note and the small heart. Write a kind message of encouragement and friendship inside the square. You may want to use the heart to write a promise coupon for something helpful you're willing to do. Decorate the note, or send it as is. To close the note, place the heart on top of the square; fold in the top and bottom flaps; then hook the two halves of the heart together.

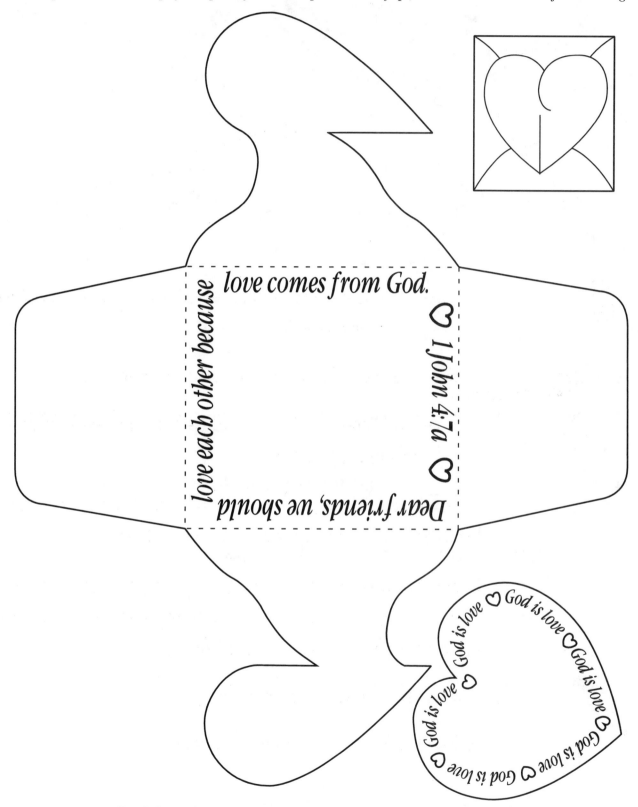

MASTERPIECE Cookies

Ready to create an edible masterpiece?

1. Spread a layer of frosting on a cookie.

2. Use the decorations available to create a design on a plate beside the cookie.

3. Once you know exactly how you want the design to look, transfer it to the cookie.

4. Make at least one more cookie masterpiece so you'll have one to eat and one to share.

5. Carefully place in a sandwich bag the cookie you plan to share.

Group Publishing, Inc.
Attention: Product Development
P.O. Box 481
Loveland, CO 80539
Fax: (970) 679-4370

Evaluation for *SUNDAY SCHOOL SPECIALS 4*

Please help Group Publishing, Inc., continue to provide innovative and useful resources for ministry. Please take a moment to fill out this evaluation and mail or fax it to us. Thanks!

● ● ●

1. As a whole, this book has been (circle one)

not very helpful   very helpful

1   2   3   4   5   6   7   8   9   10

2. The best things about this book:

3. Ways this book could be improved:

4. Things I will change because of this book:

5. Other books I'd like to see Group publish in the future:

6. Would you be interested in field-testing future Group products and giving us your feedback? If so, please fill in the information below:

Name _____

Street Address _____

City _____ State _____ ZIP _____

Phone Number _____ Date _____

BRING THE BIBLE TO LIFE FOR YOUR 1ST- THROUGH 6TH-GRADERS... WITH GROUP'S HANDS-ON BIBLE CURRICULUM™

Energize your kids with Active Learning!

Group's **Hands-On Bible Curriculum**™ will help you teach the Bible in a radical new way. It's based on Active Learning—the same teaching method Jesus used.

In each lesson, students will participate in exciting and memorable learning experiences using fascinating gadgets and gizmos you've not seen with any other curriculum. Your elementary students will discover biblical truths and <u>remember</u> what they learn because they're <u>doing</u> instead of just listening.

You'll save time and money, too!

While students are learning more, you'll be working less—simply follow the quick and easy instructions in the **Teacher Guide**. You'll get tons of material for an energy-packed 35- to 60-minute lesson. And, if you have extra time, there's an arsenal of Bonus Ideas and Time Stuffers to keep kids occupied—and learning! Plus, you'll SAVE BIG over other curriculum programs that require you to buy expensive separate student books—all student handouts in Group's **Hands-On Bible Curriculum** are photocopiable!

In addition to the easy-to-use **Teacher Guide**, you'll get all the essential teaching materials you need in a ready-to-use **Learning Lab**®. No more running from store to store hunting for lesson materials—all the active-learning tools you need to teach 13 exciting Bible lessons to any size class are provided for you in the **Learning Lab**.

Challenging topics each quarter keep your kids coming back!

Group's **Hands-On Bible Curriculum** covers topics that matter to your kids and teaches them the Bible with integrity. Switching topics every month keeps your 1st- through 6th-graders enthused and coming back for more. The full two-year program will help your kids...

- make God-pleasing decisions,
- recognize their God-given potential, and
- seek to grow as Christians.

Take the boredom out of Sunday school, children's church, and midweek meetings for your elementary students. Make your job easier and more rewarding with no-fail lessons that are ready in a flash. Order Group's **Hands-On Bible Curriculum** for your 1st- through 6th-graders today.

Hands-On Bible Curriculum is also available for Toddlers & 2s, Preschool, and Pre-K and K!

Order today from your local Christian bookstore, or write: Group Publishing, P.O. Box 485, Loveland, CO 80539.

Exciting Resources for Your Children's Ministry

No-Miss Lessons for Preteen Kids

Getting the attention of 5th- and 6th-graders can be tough. Meet the challenge with these 22 faith-building, active-learning lessons that deal with self-esteem…relationships…making choices…and other topics. Perfect for Sunday school, meeting groups, lock-ins, and retreats!

ISBN 0-7644-2015-1

The Children's Worker's Encyclopedia of Bible-Teaching Ideas

New ideas—and lots of them!—for captivating children with stories from the Bible. You get over 340 attention-grabbing, active-learning devotions…art and craft projects…creative prayers…service projects… field trips…music suggestions…quiet reflection activities…skits…and more—winning ideas from each and every book of the Bible! Simple, step-by-step directions and handy indexes make it easy to slide an idea into any meeting—on short notice—with little or no preparation!

Old Testament   ISBN 1-55945-622-1
New Testament   ISBN 1-55945-625-6

"Show Me!" Devotions for Leaders to Teach Kids

Susan L. Lingo

Here are all the eye-catching science tricks, stunts, and illusions that kids love learning so they can flabbergast adults…but now there's an even *better* reason to know them! Each amazing trick is an illustration for an "Oh, Wow!" devotion that drives home a memorable Bible truth. Your children will learn how to share these devotions with others, too!

ISBN 0-7644-2022-4

Fun & Easy Games

With these 89 games, your children will *cooperate* instead of compete—so everyone finishes a winner! That means no more hurt feelings…no more children feeling like losers…no more hovering over the finish line to be sure there's no cheating. You get new games to play in gyms…classrooms…outside on the lawn…and as you travel!

ISBN 0-7644-2042-9

Order today from your local Christian bookstore, or write: Group Publishing, P.O. Box 485, Loveland, CO 80539.

More Resources for Your Children's Ministry

Quick Children's Sermons: Will My Dog Be in Heaven?

Kids ask the most amazing questions—and now you'll be ready to answer 50 of them! You'll get witty, wise, and biblically solid answers to kid-size questions...and each question and answer makes a wonderful children's sermon. This is an attention-grabbing resource for children's pastors, Sunday school teachers, church workers, and parents.

ISBN 1-55945-612-

"Let's Play!" Group Games for Preschoolers

Make playtime learning time with great games that work in any size class! Here are more than 140 easy-to-lead, fun-to-play games that teach preschoolers about Bible characters and stories. You'll love the clear, simple directions, and your kids will love that they can actually do these games!

ISBN 1-55945-613-

More Than Mud Pies

Preschoolers love making crafts...but finished crafts are often forgotten long before the glue dries. Until now! These 48 3-D crafts become fun games your preschoolers will play again and again. And every time they play, your preschoolers will be reminded of important Bible truths. Each craft comes with photocopiable game instructions to send home to parents!

ISBN 0-7644-2044-

The Discipline Guide for Children's Ministry

Jody Capehart, Gordon West & Becki West

With this book you'll understand and implement classroom-management techniques that work—and th make teaching fun again! From a thorough explanation of age-appropriate concerns...to proven strategie for heading off discipline problems before they occur...here's a practical book you'll turn to again and again!

ISBN 1-55945-686-

Order today from your local Christian bookstore, or write: Group Publishing, P.O. Box 485, Loveland, CO 80539.